GONE

GONE

A GIRL,

A VIOLIN,

A LIFE

UNSTRUNG

MIN KYM

 CROWN
NEW YORK

Library of Congress Cataloging-in-Publication Data
Names: Kym, Min, author.
Title: Gone : a girl, a violin, a life unstrung / Min Kym.
Description: First edition. | New York : Crown, 2017.
Identifiers: LCCN 2016054104 (print) | LCCN 2016054944 (ebook) |
ISBN 9780451496072 (hardcover) | ISBN 9780451496089 (pbk.) |
ISBN 9780451496096 (ebook)
Subjects: LCSH: Kym, Min. | Violinists—Biography. |
Loss (Psychology) | LCGFT: Autobiographies.
Classification: LCC ML418.K96 A3 2017 (print) |
LCC ML418.K96 (ebook) | DDC 787.2092 [B]—dc23
LC record available at https://lccn.loc.gov/2016054104

ISBN 978-0-451-49607-2
Ebook ISBN 978-0-451-49609-6

Printed in the United States of America

Book design by Lauren Dong
Jacket design by Christopher Brand
Jacket photographs: (rip) George Baier IV; (author) Toby Jacobs

10 9 8 7 6 5 4 3 2 1

First American Edition

LISTEN AS YOU READ

Penguin Random House and Warner Classics have partnered to release an album to accompany *Gone*.

As you read, you can listen to the pieces described in the book, played by Min Kym. Most of the pieces were recorded at the time when she originally performed them, though they have now been specially remastered for this companion album. When music referred to in the book is available on the album, you will see (($\flat$)) in the page margin.

Gone: The Album has been released on Warner Classics and is available for streaming, download, and as a CD from Apple Music, Spotify, Amazon, and selected music retailers. For links and more information, visit www.gonethealbum.com.

Finally, *Gone* has also been published as an unabridged audiobook, read by Rebecca Yeo and interwoven with music from the album. It is available for download from Audible and other websites.

∽

Gone: The Album
Min Kym

GONE

I've been dreaming about my violin. I am waiting to board an airplane, maybe flying to a concert, maybe flying away from one. It's hard to say. I am alone. Maybe I should be with my mother or my old tutor. It's hard to say. My violin is with me but the woman at the check-in says it has to go down into the hold. I don't want it to go into the hold, it's never been put there before, but those are the airline's rules—or is it that I have not filled out a form properly? I have the feeling that it could all be my fault. I lift the case up and place the violin on the conveyor belt. The woman ties a label to the handle, presses her foot to start the conveyor-belt motor. The violin gives a little start, as if it's been pushed in the back, something it won't have liked, and then starts to be carried away, slowly disappearing through the rubber flaps. Do I see it tip up as it reaches the end, as if it's fallen off a cliff? I can't quite make it out, but in that instant something tells me I will never see my violin again. A little time later I am in the plane, or maybe I am out of the plane. We have flown, or we have landed, or something has happened to cause us to disembark. That's it. Something has happened to cause us to disembark. Everyone is happy that they are safe, but I know that something terrible has happened. No one will say what,

1

but something terrible has happened. An announcement comes on. There has been an explosion, in the hold. We will have to wait to find out what has happened to our luggage, which bags have been saved and which have not. We wait and we wait. No one comes to tell me whether my violin is alive or whether my violin is dead. I am alone and yet I am barely there. I've gone. I am no longer quite me. It's a worrying thought. Then I tell myself not to worry. It's a dream. There is no plane, no hold, no explosion. My violin is with me. We are safe. I am whole.

I wake up. It's not a dream at all.

1

IT STARTED LIKE THIS.

We were a Korean family, living in London. My father was a mechanical engineer working for Daewoo, before the company started making cars. It wasn't so famous then. We'd been living in England for three years. Like my older sister, I was learning English at school. At home we spoke Korean. It was perfectly natural. We'd be going home eventually.

Meanwhile, we got to learn English ways. Every week I would go with my sister to the local music school my mother had found in the Yellow Pages, and every week I would sit there, kicking my heels while my sister had her piano lesson. She was good, my sister. I would listen to her play and wonder whether it would ever be my turn. I started writing, picked up the pen with my left hand. No, I couldn't do that. I had to put my left hand behind my back, use my right. At school no one had batted an eyelid, but my mother was worried about what people would think when we went back to Korea. In Korea it was considered bad luck to be left-handed. So I became right-handed. Korea was still our final destination. We went to a Korean church, and, once a week, to a Korean school two and a half hours away. But the journey gave me nosebleeds, so my mother taught me to read and write Korean at home. It was important. Korea was where our home lay.

Then, one day, my mother asked me the question I'd been waiting for, and everything changed.

"Do you want to play?"

She'd already decided I wasn't going to play the piano. There was only one piano teacher in the school and no available slots on the day of my sister's lesson. If I chose the piano, my mother would have to accompany me on another day, and that would have defeated the whole purpose of the exercise. It had to be something else. There were only two spaces free at the same time as my sister learned her piano: a trumpet space and a violin space. The trumpet didn't appeal at all. But the violin! I leapt at the idea.

I had to wait a week, a week where the space lay open, unused, where a violin waited for me, untouched. I found it almost unbearable. The prospect gnawed at my bones. I had to do something. Before we went to bed, my sister and I would often play little games, act out little plays with each other. One of us would be a waitress, the other a customer; one of us would be a doctor, the other a patient. I always imagined, at that age, that I would be a doctor. I had been in the hospital myself and had liked the doctors who looked after me, liked the idea of growing up to be like them, helping patients get better. Now, I insisted, we would not play a game at all. We would play duets. So my sister made a paper keyboard while I copied the shape of a violin from our children's encyclopedia and cut it out. Together we played our duets. When it was over I took my violin to bed, played it some more, under the bedclothes. It was silent, but I could hear it. It weighed nothing, but I could feel it.

My best friend was also taking violin lessons. She offered to lend me her quarter-size, but it was too big. So my mother went down to the local music shop and bought a tiny eight-size violin. It was a harsh, factory-made thing from China, but when I held it I could feel the romance within. I had a history of teaching myself to play instruments. I'd taught myself the piano, recorder and harmonica. By the time the day came around, I'd worked out how to play "Twinkle, Twinkle, Little Star."

It might have been then, on my first lesson, or it might have been my second; it's hard to pinpoint the exact moment, but let me say that I knew right away that holding a violin, playing a violin, was not simply *for* me, but it *was* me. Everything about it seemed so easy, so natural; the way it settled on my body, my fingers so utterly comfortable in that position. There was nothing awkward or alien about it at all: my arm stretched out, my hand grasped the neck, my chin and shoulder pressed to the body, my legs firm on the floor. There was a normality to it that seemed completely familiar. I knew I could play anything. Anything. This was not arrogance— I was a shy child, reluctant to come forward, to give voice, to take center stage—but more simply that I had found, not only my home and my voice, but my element. I could swim in this world. I could dive and soar. I could ride crests and float down streams, swim with or against any current. I felt like a creature released, alive in herself for the first time.

There was a problem. I was shown how to work the big horsehair bow with the nub of rosin, shown how the hard nut transformed into a soft, white powder, covering the strands and seeping into the air. The bow thus oiled, I found out how to draw the sound out, how you had to coax it. But the rosin gave me asthma. I was allergic to it, wasn't able to play for more than half an hour before being felled by a terrible wheezing, my chest seized in an iron grip, my lungs convulsed, fighting for air that wasn't there. I was put on steroids to keep the attacks at bay. But rather than being a hindrance, my asthma became an indication of my talent. I couldn't practice like anyone else, couldn't put the hours in. But it didn't hold me back. I could still progress; progress at a rate that was way outside the norm. Asthma, the potentially debilitating nature of it, became a mark of my agility, a badge denoting a child who possessed unusual skill. Other children got asthma. Only, mine proved I was unlike the others. It marked me out.

I swam fast now, immersed in my element. I reached Grade 2 in the first eight weeks, and a month later came Grade 4. I know it sounds unlikely, but that's how quick and easy it was for me. It was just a natural thing to do. I picked it up. I played. My only frustration was the sound that was coming out of the wood: I knew it could be better. My goal right away was not to sound like a baby. I wanted a grown-up voice, instinctively knew the difference, knew what a grown-up voice was, how it should be. The ear was the driving force, not the fingers. The fingers were merely muscle and bone. The playing—what it is, what it should be, what it must be—came from the ear. The ear was my element too. I had perfect pitch.

I had always lived in a world of sound. I can hardly remember a time when I could not read music. My mother claims she never taught me, and I certainly don't remember learning. What I do remember is my father coming back from a business trip and bringing with him a little xylophone, the name of each key—A, B-flat, B, C—painted on the colored slats. Perhaps that's how I learned. Certainly the words of music became my favored language, how I heard the world, interpreted it. A bicycle ring was an E-flat. The squeak of a door, C major. When I heard people talk, I listened to the rhythm of their voices, their inflections, rather than the matter of their actual words.

Grade 2, Grade 4, it sounds like hard work. It was work, I suppose, but it was mainly fun. I could do it. My teacher probably pushed me, but I was never aware of it. Lessons weren't lessons, they were little journeys, every one different, every one leading to a new destination. We played duets. He called me his little assistant as I went around the class, tuning all the other pupils' instruments. I was the youngest in a class of ten. He understood that, above all, I was a perfectionist, that it mattered absolutely to me, the sound that came out, that it was never just about the notes. He made me think of music as a story. Most of the pieces I played with him—Wieniawski's *Légende*, Elgar's *Salut d'Amour*—he'd tell me a story, and where there wasn't one, I would make one up, cobble tales and myths together, Icarus flying too close to the sun. ((♪1))

He would give me records, on birthdays, holidays, Christmas; not all violin music, but always classical music, always food for my ears. Beethoven's Fourth was like a schoolgirl crush, I fell in love with it so hard. There were others, but the one that stood out, the one that confirmed everything that I already believed in, was the double album by Austrian-born violinist Fritz Kreisler. I had never heard of Kreisler before, knew nothing of the legend that surrounded him, never fully understood (although I think I knew it deep in my heart) the magnitude of what a violin, the right violin, could offer. But hearing Kreisler play was when I heard the evidence of the possible; when I realized what the violin was truly capable of, that it had a voice, a personality, a view of things. Kreisler showed me how it lived and breathed and raised its soul to the heavens. I listened to his recording of Brahms and Beethoven, but also his own compositions, the *Liebesleid*, the *Liebesfreude* and the *Schön Rosmarin*, and pieces of utter charm such as Dvořák's *Humoresque* No. 7. I played them over and over again, never tiring, only wondering at the great marvel of Kreisler being Kreisler; how his playing *was* Kreisler: how his violin was Kreisler, how every note he played was Kreisler. Maybe it was then that I understood that I had a voice of my own too.

By this time I had graduated from my factory Chinese violin to a better-made quarter-size. I was both sorry and relieved to say goodbye to it—though it has never really left me. I have it still. It was, and still is, a part of me, as are all the violins I have owned. I have kept them all—all except one.

My sister had graduated from our little music school to the Purcell School in Harrow on the Hill. Like the time of her music lessons, I grew envious of her age. She was nine; I was seven. She'd come back with grown-up tales of singing in the choir, of playing music all day, and there I was, languishing in my ordinary school with my meager weekly violin lessons. I longed for release. Then, one day an unexpected opportunity came. I was with my mother at the Purcell School, collecting my sister. I had my little violin with me. The headmaster, John Bain, was there. He said, "Can you play that?" He asked it as a kind, indulgent question any grown-up might ask a little girl, but I took it as a request. Certainly I could. I took out my violin and played. I played Bach's Concerto in A minor. After I finished he said he thought he might be able to bend the rules: I would be allowed in two years earlier than usual. And considering the burden on my parents, he would see what he could do about financial help.

One brief hour on one afternoon and the future suddenly shone ahead. I could almost see it.

I was already living in two worlds, the world of music and my other life at school. Or was it three: music, school and home? Our home life was certainly very different from everyone else's. As young children, my sister and I would never start our meal until our father had finished. When we had finished, then would come our mother's turn. Father first, children second, mother last: that was the immovable Korean order. Other things that seemed perfectly normal to us would have perplexed and outraged our friends. If I wanted to drink a glass of water, I would ask permission. It wasn't a question of being refused a glass of water, it was a question of respect, of acknowledging the pecking order. It ran from top to bottom. My father wouldn't let my mother drive. She would have liked to, but he was adamant. His word ruled, but we hardly saw him. By the time we woke up, he would have already gone to work. By the time he came back, we were already in bed. On the weekends he'd be off to play golf, so we didn't see him then either. He was a remote but kind man, with a deep and sometimes fearsome voice. My mother's voice was warm and funny but with an unpredictable edge of volatility to it. She cooked and fed us all, did the housework and lived alone, with a distant husband. After a night's drinking he'd often come back late with colleagues, expecting her to cook a small banquet for his guests. And she would be proud to do so. It was the Korean way.

It wasn't a question of right or wrong, it was simply how things were done; the man, the woman, the children. And children, I think, were seen in a peculiar light: loved, but in a way not quite human, not exactly objects or dolls, but with an element of malleability within them, to be moved about, or not. My mother would leave me alone quite a lot. She'd take my sister to the doctor or go out shopping and leave me alone, no concept of time in my head, no idea when or whether she was coming back. I'd hide behind the curtains, heart pounding, petrified that someone might knock on the door. It wouldn't happen now, but back in the eighties it was quite a normal thing to do among the ex-pat mothers; Korean mores asserting their influence. Korean children were required to show much more independence than children in the West. Back home there was nothing unusual in seeing children— some no older than four—walking to school on their own.

I went to the local state primary school. I'd made friends with a girl down the road. I liked my classmates well enough; they were friendly and I enjoyed learning new things together. But being the only Korean family in the community, my sister and I stood out. My sister in her new school seemed to handle this better than me. I saw her blossom and grow in confidence and I longed to become as much a part of this new world as she seemed to be. One morning, at an assembly at my own school, the headmistress put on a record. It was folk music. Some of the bigger boys and girls had prepared a dance and I was captivated. I felt the music working its way inside me, taking shape. Suddenly I felt a tap on my shoulder, a voice in my ear:

"What's wrong with you? Do you want to dance or something?"

It was one of the big boys. I could hear the sarcasm. Mortified, I realized that I'd been moving to the music. My cheeks burned. Everyone was looking at me. I shrank back and took hold of myself. After that, whenever I heard music I would take great care to check that I wasn't moving to it, to restrain myself. But now I told myself all that would soon be over—I would be going to a music school where there would be others like me who played musical instruments, and where it didn't matter if I moved to the music. That's what music did: it moved you. One way or another it got you going, inside, outside, every side. And it was going to be my world, my coming world!

And, suddenly, it was wrenched away.

We had been living in England for over four years when my father had to return to South Korea. We flew back. We come from a big family—both my mother and father are one of seven, and they were as pleased to see our relations as the family were to see us. My sister seemed happy enough too. Korea was buzzing with excitement, for it had been recently announced that the 1988 Olympics would be held there. The country had been granted the worldwide legitimacy that it had craved for so long. But for me our return spelled misery. I had returned to a life I didn't know, an ordered, regulated, Korean life.

My sister and I were enrolled in the local school. I didn't tell anyone that I'd just come from England. In those days, people didn't leave Korea—to leave Korea was wrong—and I didn't want to stand out. I got a little bullied when the news leaked out. "Why were you exported to England? What are you? A packet of noodles?" I made friends with two girls. They showed me the ways of the Korean playground, the hierarchy of it, how to avoid getting into trouble by obeying the rules and never, ever forgetting your homework. Corporal punishment was still the norm in Korea, and I saw how a teacher would call a pupil up to the front of the class and give them a hefty thwack on their outstretched hand with a wooden switch. My friends taught me how I was not to ever address an older girl or boy by their first name, how I had to call them either "older brother" or "older sister," even though there was nothing brotherly or sisterly about it. (With anyone younger, you could be as rude as you liked. I felt indignant about that, being the youngest in my family.) Every morning we had to march up and down like soldiers. We were taught how to salute the flag, hold our hands behind our backs. We sang Korean hymns, everything in uniform. We wore little slippers (it's considered uncouth to wear shoes indoors). Before we could eat, we would wash our feet. It was very different from life in my primary school back in England, a complete shift. So, I went to school. I came home, did my homework, lots of it. On the weekends the shift continued— an endless stream of family events, outings, get-togethers, all governed by duties and rules. You greeted an elder, you knelt at their feet. Western incredulity would spring unwanted into my mind: "What is this?" But there was no choice in the matter. Korea is a family-oriented society and respect is all.

The violin I brought with me rarely came out and when it did, it was a disaster. My mother, trying her utmost, found me a teacher, an hour and a half and two bus rides away; the violin strapped to my back, my mother carrying the heavy case of music. The teacher seemed a nice enough woman, but completely inappropriate to my needs. She'd never been outside Korea and had no feeling for the music that lived within me. The work she knuckled me down to was not what music was about—the *feel* of it—but a question of scales and fingering. Regulation, in other words: correct order, uniformity, above everything. If I lifted my finger off the bow, it was seen not as natural movement that was expressing the physique of the player, or the state of the violin, or the sudden mood of the music, but as a challenge to her authority. After a few lessons it dawned on me that she had not played a single note herself. Could she even *play* the violin? I wondered. Then one day I asked her if she wouldn't mind showing me what she meant rather than telling me. She flew into a rage, and though I tried to hide it, tears pricked my eyes. She yelled at me some more. The lesson ended. Afterward, my mother rebuked me for my backchat, reminding me that we weren't in England anymore. She knew I hadn't meant to be impertinent, but I had to understand—I couldn't question or challenge my teachers like that. I was in Korea now.

We never went back, didn't look for another teacher. It was recognized that it would be better for me to have no violin lessons at all than to go through those which only served to heighten my sense of loss. So the violin gathered dust, and, when I took it out, it felt empty, neglected, bereft—as did I. This was a new kind of unhappiness: not unhappiness for the lack of love, not unhappiness caused by fear and uncertainty, but an overwhelming denial of the spirit, of my voice. I had never imagined such a thing could happen, that something so strong could empty your childish frame, deny you your reason for being. How could I? Yet it did. However young my years, I knew I was dying inside, the balance of me gone. For six months I died and I died. After a while it didn't seem to matter. Apart from my violin nothing did. I was resigned to fading into nothingness. That was all right. Soon, I wouldn't exist at all.

How long it would have gone on for, whether I would have recovered without the next turn of events, is impossible to know. It's difficult to imagine another way out. But it happened. My father was posted to Libya, a country in constant flux. It was obvious we would not be going with him. My mother had two choices: to stay in Korea or to return to England. Staying in Korea was a perfectly good option for her and my sister. But for me it spelled catastrophe and, in their hearts, my parents knew it. My future, the future that they could see, had already taken embryonic shape. John Bain at the Purcell School had been better than his word. The school got in touch: did I still want to join the next term? They'd written to the Home Secretary explaining the situation, outlining my prospects, had arranged for a full government scholarship and a permanent residency visa for us all. Their desire for me to enroll couldn't have been set out more clearly. It was an indication of what they thought of me, an indication not lost on my parents. Even so, it was not an easy decision for them to make, to pack up our belongings once more, leave Korea, return to the strangeness of the West. This wasn't to further the head of the family's career. This would be done on the behalf of the youngest member of the family, and a girl at that. The rest of the family were deeply opposed, for historical reasons as much as anything else. It's hard perhaps for Westerners to imagine the state of paranoia South Korea labored under in those days. My grandparents' generation were survivors of the Korean War, and the scars ran long and deep.

All my grandparents had spent their early life in a Korea that was not divided, in a Korea that—although occupied by Japan—was whole. My grandfather on my mother's side was descended from an aristocratic family, the Yu, and he was their youngest son. The family had lived in a huge country house of eighty rooms, passed down from generation to generation. Rice and watermelons were grown on the land. In Korea in those days—much as in England, I suspect—the eldest son inherited everything, with the understanding that he would look after his parents and grandparents. The younger son or sons got nothing. So my grandfather became something of an entrepreneur. He was charismatic, a fantastic salesman, understood business, was always trying to find the trade that would set him up and support his family. When the war came, he went into hiding, deep into the jungle. Being the son of a landowner, he'd have been first in line for reprisals, taken prisoner, executed. He was thirty and had five children by this time, my mother being the youngest. He had to find some way to support them all. He learned how to make clothes.

In 1951 my mother was living with her siblings and my grandmother in their house in the country. It was strafed by enemy aircraft and my grandmother sustained a bad leg wound. The leg became infected, gangrenous. Everyone thought my grandmother would die and her young child would die with her (for how could they support a baby?). A grave was readied and a shroud thrown over their bodies. But my mother's elder brother, who was about twelve, had other ideas. He'd always been a voracious reader and had read somewhere that the way to stop gangrene was to cut the offending limb off. So that's what he did. With the help of an older man, he found a bottle of whiskey, forced his mother to drink half of it, and then helped saw her leg off—his own mother's leg. She lost a great deal of blood but, though very weak, recovered. When the news of my grandmother's plight reached my grandfather he used the connections he'd made to obtain some penicillin and have it sent over. This was the clincher that saved her life, but she was still weak, unable to look after my mother. My uncle took charge again. He would go down to the nearby pond, catch frogs, feed her those. The end of the war brought peace, but not much else. They'd lost everything: their big house in the country, their land, their money. As she grew up, her own mother disabled, my mother became a mother to her younger siblings born after the war, clothed them, fed them, made sure they went to school. She was very resourceful, had a relentless/entrepreneurial spirit of her own. Little wonder the ties were so strong.

My father came from the Kim dynasty. Kim is a common name in Korea. In old Korea, each king would name his personal servants after his own name. Kim was a successful king, had a lot of servants. My father was a child when the war ended, had lost his own father, who had been an engineer working on the railways, when he was three years old. When he died, my father went to live with his uncle. The uncle was the head of the house. His word was law. Every day he'd send his nephews out to catch fish for supper. My father went with them, though, aged five, there wasn't a lot of fishing he could do—can't remember if he ever caught any. What he does remember, though, is coming back with the catch and seeing his uncle take the fish and divide the spoils between the elders. The boys wouldn't get any, were just fed on the scraps that were left over. But that was the culture in Korea (and still is, to an extent). Elders are important. Elders matter. Children are very much second-class citizens.

So, they had tough childhoods, and the specter of North Korea—what it might do—was still very much alive, even years later. There were daily exhortations on buses to be wary of spies, warnings of child kidnappings. There was nothing North Korea couldn't or wouldn't do. To the family, the idea of my mother whisking me away abroad again, away from their protective arms, smacked of the North's worst excesses of abduction and brainwashing. Defying their fears would only serve to widen the divide.

Yes, I was unhappy—it was the wrong place for me to be—but there were times when I did forget that feeling: the days I spent with my grandmother. I lived with her for many months. She would always watch the soap operas set in the past. She had a longing for the old Korean ways. I guess it's the same for many people of her age, wherever they come from, their love for their country's old habits. The new Korea that sprang up after the war was foreign to her, a cacophony of wire and concrete obliterating swathes of what she had known. You have to go quite deep in now to get a sense of the real beauty of the Korean countryside, the heady blossoms that abound, the density and peace of the greenery. In the endless cities that have sprung up, all that has gone. So my grandmother lived in the country, always. I loved going there.

She kept her house very much in the Korean tradition: all on one floor, quite high up, so you'd walk up the steps and into the body of it. The front room looked out across to the mountains. There was a feeling of space and quiet and ages past. It was comfortable, the heating coming up through the floor. The basement was home to a piping-hot stove and a great stack of coal, and it was a constant job to fill the stove with the large compressed disks. It was a serious (and dangerous) mission to go down there, for there was the constant threat of carbon-monoxide poisoning.

Grandmother was a calligrapher and had taught herself tapestry; she would make beautiful silk needleworks, most of which told a tale. Perhaps that is where I got the feel for my playing. My mother still has a screen relating the story of a marriage. First the young boy and girl are introduced; the next scene they're getting married; the next they have children. It's highly stylized, highly idealized, but that's how it was. There were stages. You went through them. You didn't question it. My mother and father, for instance, had an arranged marriage. My father lived with his eldest brother and his wife, and, naturally, with my grandmother (remember, the eldest son *always* looked after the parents). It was important to them they found my father a suitable wife. They lived across from my mother's older sister, shared a garden with them. My grandmother started talking to her over the fence: "Oh, I have a good-looking son who . . ."; "Oh, I have a pretty younger sister who . . ."; just an everyday Korean conversation. They had the same social standing, or near enough in the fractured Korea of the fifties. The families decided to set them up. Nothing would have been done if they had disliked each other, but then again, that sense of one's own personality, of listening to how you yourself felt, was very much on the back foot. Self had little to do with it. What was required topped it every time. It sounds incredible to put this down on paper, but my mother married my father *without knowing his first name*. She was so shy that for a long time she couldn't bring herself to ask him what it might be. It's hard to comprehend the nuts and bolts of that, hard to imagine the circumstances that would develop from it. How could you *not* know your husband's name? Was she disappointed when she found out what it was? When I ask her now, "What did you talk about?" she smiles and says, "We just sat there, looking at each other." Trying to put a face to a name, perhaps.

That's what Korean life was, structure: structured courtship, structured marriage, and a family run on highly structured lines, the world my grandmother came from and one to which she clung fiercely. It wasn't a matter of being old-fashioned. It was a matter of *being*—although she didn't quite understand the concept of the telephone, thought it more like a tape recorder, didn't quite grasp the fact that there was another live person at the end of it. If you called her up she would listen to what you said, then hang up. It became a running family joke.

The Purcell School was still anxious to know if I was going to take up their offer. My mother wavered back and forth, pulled by conflicting loyalties, loyalty to the family, loyalty to me. We received another letter. The Associated Board Grade 4 that I had taken before we left had been given the highest mark in the country that year (147 out of 150), and I was going to be given a prize for it. If we could do nothing else, it would be lovely if I could return, if only briefly, just to accept it in person. That letter seemed to tip the balance, confirmation that there was the possibility of something special lying within me. Maybe going back to England wasn't such a crazy idea after all. My father stepped in. A man so used to playing his ordained role, maintaining the rules and regulations of Korean family law, now ripped those rules apart and chose the call of the Western world outside them. "I don't care what the family thinks," he said. "We have to do this." For a man of his background and temperament, it was an extraordinarily bold thing to say and act upon. My debt to him lies embedded in these words.

My mother called a friend who lived in Harrow. We could stay there for a few days while she found somewhere to live. Armed with two suitcases, we left everything behind, flew out of Korea on Korean Airlines. It was before the days they were allowed to fly across Soviet airspace, and we stopped off in Alaska, ate a bowl of noodles in the airport while the plane refueled. There was sadness in the air; I could see it in my mother's quiet face, a mixed bowl of emotions: hope, fortitude, loss. The plane might have carried us, but it was my violin that had given us wings. Although I was the reason for us going, she didn't have much time for me. During the flight my sister was horribly sick. We landed at Heathrow and took a number 140 bus. My mum scoured the newspapers and found a house to rent in Greenford, just off the A40 in northwest London. We moved in two days before the start of the new term at the Purcell School. No furniture, makeshift cutlery, disposable plates, we started from scratch, sleeping on the floor, living on cups of soup. In the bedroom at the back, where I practiced, I could look out the window and see the driving range of the golf course.

My violin and I were coming home. Soon I would be able to take it out of its case, look it in the face again. Soon we'd be playing, our feet on the ground but travelers in the world of music. But it was always in the back of my mind, the sacrifices the family was making. My mother was leaving her husband, her home, leaving against the advice and wishes of everyone close to her, taking a chance on something, taking a chance on me. I was the reason this was happening. I was the reason she and my sister were forsaking everything that was safe, and understood, where life's lines and life's expectations were clearly drawn. What if it didn't work out? What if *I* didn't work out? Did I say that then? Of course not. I wouldn't have even known the words, but it was already there, a little hard core of determination fused with ability lying within me— Min, the cold, hard reason for it all.

And my violin? Now my violin was not simply my voice, my reason, but my savior too. One day, when I was older, I would have a violin that was truly my own, a violin who would guide and protect me forever.

Greenford was our home for about a year. The thing I remember most about it is that it was at Greenford where my eyesight started going wrong. There was a lamppost outside my bedroom window, and though my mother would turn the lights out (as parents do), I would sit up and read by the light outside. One day, as I was practicing, I realized I couldn't make out the definition of the trees out by the golf course anymore. I had completely ruined my eyes. I became a girl with glasses.

The first day of the new school, my mother had forgotten how to get there. In desperation, we hired a mini-cab. It was late, as was our arrival. For the first time I felt nervous. Every day started with us singing. That day, like every other, we were given music to sight-read and sing. Our teacher, Anne Osborn, listened to us one by one. When it came to my turn, I couldn't get a single note out. Eventually, in the kindest possible way, she suggested that I sing along with my sister, like our bedtime paper duets but with sound. I took a deep breath. Out they came. After that, my confidence returned. Miss Osborn cultivated an appreciation and understanding of choral music that has informed my playing ever since. Every first Wednesday of the month we would go to Evensong with the Harrow Boys at St. Mary's, reputed to be one of the oldest churches in England and where, by the graveyard, Byron used to sit. I loved the choir, loved the concerts we gave. As with my earliest teacher, I became the school's tuning fork. "Give us an A," Miss Osborn would say. I would sing my A and the show would begin.

My first violin teacher at the Purcell School was Jean Fiske. She had auburn hair, whisked up into a Dusty Springfield–type bouffant beehive. She was inquisitive, with soft, kindly eyes, yet had something of a steely detective within her, searching you out, seeing your weaknesses and your strengths. Jean told me that she didn't think she'd be able to take me much beyond a year. A little girl like me— and here was a woman, with her grown-up arms and her grown-up legs, telling me that she would not be enough for me, that I would outgrow her. I'd just returned to my land of music and in twelve months I would outgrow her! Already it was being made very clear to me what they thought I was, what they thought I would become. There were people there ready to tower over me, raise their arms, water my talent, see it blossom and grow, and I suppose I could feel the stirrings of that expectation too, whatever it was, growing inside me. I was the youngest in the school, but my violin and I were growing fast beyond my years.

The Purcell School wasn't used to someone like me. I was too young, too quick. I wasn't exactly an experiment, but the headmaster told my parents that they had learned a lot from me being there, how to handle young aptitude. It wasn't a race the school was holding, but I was overtaking things, pupils, teachers. Couldn't help it. It's how I was, what I was made of. I looked ordinary but somewhere there was a different fuel burning within me. That was all right, but it brought its responsibilities, its duties. I was always the one asked to represent the school, always the one chosen to perform. John Bain was asked to choose a couple of pupils to play at a rapprochement meeting between Margaret Thatcher and Ted Heath, which took place at the Savoy. I can't remember what I played, and quite why we went; never knew, never asked. Why would I? It was becoming a given. The school had its own PR department, and I was a central part of it. Without choosing, without questioning, without hardly noticing, I had become a kind of mascot. And mascots may be alive, but they aren't quite real. They're brushed and preened and paraded forth. They stand for something else, not themselves.

There was a lot happening. My father came back from Libya once every four months, the distance growing between us not simply measured in miles. My teachers were closer to me than him. My mother was on her own, anxious about her two children, anxious about her husband caught up in the volatile uncertainty of Gaddafi's crazed Libya. She was learning English, as were we all, but my sister and I were learning a lot quicker, a lot easier. It felt right to us. It felt strange to her. My mother spoke halted, broken English; I spoke reluctant, broken Korean. English sounds were buzzing in my head, taking shape and color. There was a mismatch my sister and I found difficult to express. If you're the product of parents who were war children, and you are aware of what happened to them, the hardships they underwent, it does make you think twice about your own conditions. My sister and I grew up thinking, "No, we can't complain. We've got it pretty good," all of which was true. We did. No leg-chopping or frog-eating for us. Just a warm, comfortable home and two parents who loved us.

But home life, Korean, was different from school life, English. At home I lived in a world governed by obedience. There were rules, the right way of doing things, for everything. It wasn't a hard way or a bad way. It was our way. We bowed when greeting each other. Not surprisingly, to live like this in England could be not only confusing, but not quite right. And I was getting a different message about this world of acceptance at school. In school I was told: "It's good to question! It's good to challenge, to find your voice." At home I was given quite the opposite. So I learned not to upset the balance between those two worlds, to tread the connecting boards lightly, without a murmur, and that was not always easy. I liked living in England. The more I learned about it, the more I liked being here. I was fascinated by Elizabeth I. I've tried to show you the sort of Korea I came from. Imagine then what effect the story of that queen might have on a well-brought-up Korean girl like me. The message I was getting from my parents was that eventually I'd find a nice husband and marry well. A Korean boy no less! You might live in England but don't make the mistake of thinking that you're English. You're Korean and you will do as Koreans do. It was an assumption that I and my sister were well aware of. England hadn't seeped into their skin. Yet I was learning about a woman who had led this country hundreds of years ago, *and who didn't marry at all*! Hearing all these new things, seeing all these new things, how men and women behaved so differently here, strengthened that sense of division, that divide between Min the violin and Min the daughter, the child, the sister.

I was being pulled in different directions, but I knew one thing. There was no way I was going to go back, grow up a woman in Korea. Two Mins, yes, but one violin. I would listen to the violin. There were voices all around me, but I was beginning to exist in a world without explanations, without sharing, a world of givens, without the fluid discourse of speech. More and more my violin alone spoke for me. Listen to the violin. Hear what the violin has to say. Technique was gathering pace, my ear ever attuned to new possibilities. I could ride those waves, swim with that current. As long as I had my violin, I had no fear. The violin would set me on the right track. The violin would lead me through.

Two concert pieces I played at this time stand out, both illustrating technique and emotion, and both asking questions of the young player. The first was Kreisler's *Schön Rosmarin*. The *Rosmarin* requires a more sophisticated technique than simple bowing. The *Rosmarin* requires what we call a flying staccato, where the bow bounces along the string in the same upbow stroke. Gravity controls it, but for it to work it has to be spontaneous, not metronomic. Listen to Kreisler, hear how, through the constant pulse, he plays around the timing, the lightness of his thought, the flutterings of the emotion, the flights of fancy he portrays—a young man remembering the image of the girl he fell in love with, the first bloom of youth. Kreisler's fingers are right on the pulse.

The second was Massenet's *Méditation*, a different piece altogether. It's taken from his opera *Thaïs* and is an instrumental interlude (written for solo violin and orchestra) that is played between the opening scenes of Act Two. Thaïs, a hedonistic courtesan in the court of Alexander the Great, has been urged to leave her life of dissolution and seek salvation through God. It is at this moment, when Thaïs is reflecting on what has been said, that the *Méditation* is played. It starts with a D-major arpeggio—the key of hope—except

(($\flat$2))

here there is a dreamlike quality evoked by the harp. Two such arpeggios set the scene and then the violin comes in on the F-sharp, a long stretch of a note which descends as the arpeggios rise and fall. It's a darker story than the Kreisler, asks for a different corner of your thoughts. The *Méditation* is one of the most beautiful pieces in the violinist's repertoire, and is very often played as an encore. I was too young to appreciate the full depth of the story, but even at that young age, it moved me to tears. You're not giving out here, you're drawing the audience in, bringing the inner world of your emotion closer to their heart. It's your own heart you should be playing by, not your memory, your own heart playing the poetry that lies within the music. When you can reach that, then everything else follows. And in that Massenet, in those first long bows, at that moment, at that concert, within that piece, a piece I had read about and practiced and played, I felt everything fall away, until there was no barrier, just the music surging inside me, drawing them in.

I took my bow and left the stage. I had made a presence and I knew it. Everything I had learned and aimed for had flown out of me and taken shape in the auditorium. I had stood with my violin and we had done what we were meant to do, what we were *built* to do. This was how it was going to be now. My path had been laid out, not only by my mother, my teachers and by me, but by my violin. I never went through that time when I asked myself, "What shall I do with myself?" Never. My violin had answered that question for me. I'd been told what I could be, and now my violin and I knew it to be true. In two years I was to be a world-class violin soloist. It wasn't a burden. It wasn't even a demand. It was my life.

I was eight and a half years old.

"WHAT'S IT LIKE TO BE A CHILD PRODIGY?"

We're eight, or five, or seven. We race ahead (of course we do). We are child prodigies. We can't help it. That's what we are. We don't ask for it (we don't train to be it), haven't been driven by ambition (not yet). We are child prodigies, cuckoos in the nest, oddities, freaks. Later, when we go to music school or college, we might meet someone who is like us, who has lived through the same experiences (there won't be many), but in the meantime we are on our own. No matter the love and support we get from our families or friends, no matter the guidance from our tutors, we are on our own. We're not *like* anyone else. Yes, we can ride a bike or play in the streets, watch TV or jump in the pool, but we are also child prodigies with an ability outside all that. Maybe it will peter out, maybe we'll crash and burn, maybe turn out to be the best exponent since . . . since the last one, who knows? We are child prodigies. We don't quite know it yet, but there's a long way to go.

What's it like to be a child prodigy? There are photographs of us everywhere. I look at photographs of Ruggiero Ricci, a child prodigy at seven. There he is, in some sort of tunic and his pageboy haircut, holding a violin which seems as big as he is, and I think of my own pictures, in my best frock, the violin huge in my hands. It's all there in his picture, in mine, the hopes, the demands, the length of time that now lies ahead. It's not a picture of a child. It's a picture of expectation, and the picture is just the start. You're a child prodigy. You could be allowed to play on your own (my mother did not recognize my skill, and had to be persuaded by my teacher that it was so), learn bad habits, play as others play, wander down an undisciplined, childish road, but you will not be. You are there to be put on show. You will be trained, perfected and pushed out on to the stage. Maybe not pushed. More likely you'll go willingly, but go you will. It is what you are expected to do and you do it. You are a child prodigy and the adult world is awaiting your presence.

What's it like to be a child prodigy? For a start there's an embarrassment, to be able to pick things up, to be a natural and yet quite unnatural. There's that peculiar sensation of feeling completely normal within yourself, but acutely aware that you are different. Somehow, you have to bridge that gap, so that in your mind you're not. People look at you and see you, not as a child, but as a child *prodigy*. You become aware of that. You form a dual personality. I formed a dual personality—not a dual nature but two personalities: the performing personality (the child prodigy), and the one that comes out to take part in everyday life (the child). But I came from a family that had nothing to do with the musical world, which meant that the two worlds were separated from one another as by a cultural wall. That was difficult. Retreating became one way of dealing with it, not putting myself forward, disguising my "prodiginess" as much as possible. But then came the question, Well, who *are* you then, if not a child prodigy? There were these groups in my school where we had to talk about our feelings, say positive things about each other: "I like so-and-so because . . ." Without fail every week everybody would say, "Well, I like Min because she's good at the violin," and I would think, "That's not a quality. Maybe people don't see me beyond that." Introversion became a shield, as, paradoxically, did the thing that had turned me into this child prodigy: my violin.

What's it like to be a child prodigy? Yes, I could do things that others could not, but with it came other adult pressures—a sense of responsibility. The better you get, the more child prodiginess you show. Your responsibilities take root, flower—to your parents, your tutors, the time everyone has invested in you, the financial outlay (not to mention the financial prospects at the end of the road). Great expectations, indeed. You start to carry a burden on your shoulders, a burden that your violin is responsible for, and only it can alleviate.

Writing this I am reminded of an interview I gave just before a recital in Spain. I have the article before me now. The questioner asks me, "What's it like to be a child prodigy?" and writes: "Min just looked at me blankly, clearly not understanding the meaning of the word." I remember thinking, even then, "No, no, no. You've misinterpreted me. I looked at you blankly because I was thinking, 'How can I answer a question like that?'" It's the question you dread, chasms of thought and doubt and confusion opening up at your feet.

So I said nothing. And someone piped up, "Well, what's extraordinary about Min is how normal she is."

This is normal?

No, this isn't normal. I was not normal, but I tried to be. Being a child prodigy was not something I wanted to wear like a badge. I felt like an alien. I'd look in the mirror and think I looked like an alien (and my Korean features didn't help either). So I would try to mingle, blend in, not stick out. Min and not Min. A child prodigy.

2

LIFE GOT SERIOUS. AFTER GRADE 4, THERE WAS A CHANGE of direction. For one thing, no more grades. Jean said, Let's not do that, let's just play. Practice became (and still is) constant, but exams had become irrelevant.

Practice isn't simply about the hours you put in. It's about concentration. The great violinist Jascha Heifetz once said in an interview that if any professional violinist needs to practice more than a couple of hours a day, then they shouldn't be one. That became a sort of mantra. Physical practice is mostly about muscle memory. Your fingers and muscles need to be able to provide a reliable vehicle for the music. So you practice, but long after you stop playing, it's still reverberating at the back of your head. You're always aware of those patterns forming. But the big thing to take away from practicing is learning not to waste time. It's so easy to waste time; we all know that. Anybody who's ever studied for a stack of exams knows how easy it is, making those timetables, those color-coded charts, putting off the hour when you have to get down to the nitty-gritty. You can do that with a violin too, faff around with it, waste time. So practicing is all about learning how to get straight to it, doing your warm-up, getting into that headspace and really focusing, really, really concentrating. It's preparing you for what lies ahead, for when you're out on stage, facing your concert audience, raising the bow for those first opening bars. That's what you will be doing: concentrating hard for one hour and forty-five minutes, a long, demanding time, physically and mentally.

And the minute you let that concentration slip, that's when mistakes happen. You're suddenly gone and, realizing it, you're a little bit jolted as you desperately lurch back in. That's when it happens: the foot fault, the missed hit. And if it doesn't, if you fit right back in the groove, you have another problem to contend with. Your mind has wandered away, and coming back you think, "Who's been playing while I've been away? *What* have they been playing while I've been away?" So, an intensity of perseverance was all. I was taking a combination of medicines—homeopathic drops, Chinese herbs, as well as conventional medicines—to keep my asthma under control. Nothing was allowed to get in the way of the violin, of the life planned ahead.

I got my first proper violin—a little half-size handmade Italian masterpiece by Vincenzo Panormo which was lent out to players who show promise. Panormo was an Italian luthier, born in Sicily in the 1730s, studied in Naples and then moved to Paris. When the French Revolution broke out he moved to Dublin, and then London, where he worked until his death. He's considered one of the greatest violin makers, strongly influenced by Stradivari and Amati. The Panormo I was loaned is a famous violin, a rare violin. Young players tend to grow out of these smaller instruments very quickly (as I did mine), so craftsmen such as Panormo tended not to expend too much of their genius in making them. This Panormo was one of perhaps half a dozen that he made.

The Panormo was a revelation, for, unlike listening to Kreisler and *his* violin, it showed me not only what a great violin might sound like, but also what I could do with it. With a great violin you begin to welcome the geography of the violin, to appreciate its anatomy. At its most obvious, the violin is shaped like a human torso, albeit a small one. It has a head, which we call the scroll. It has a neck and it has a body, a front and a back. There is a spine, which like the human spine transmits messages. The violin's spine is the sound post, connecting the front to the back. Good violins are made from a variety of wood. The back is usually maple, but maple is too unforgiving for the front. The front needs something more resonant, usually spruce. Directly above the sound post lies the bridge, and within the bridge you have apertures known as the heart and the kidneys. A low heart yields a completely different sound than a high one. Different-sized kidneys alter the sound too. When you draw your bow across the strings, the strings are pushed down onto the bridge, causing the vibrations to travel down the sound post into the body of the violin. Now full, the violin vibrates. You feel it. It's like having a cat purring. The sound vibrates within the body and disperses through the F-holes, the violin's lungs, into the air. That's what you feel: you breathe with the violin, with the phrase. You are singing through the instrument. It floats, it soars, it plunges, it poises on the cusp. It whispers, it pleads, it lets forth torrents. It possesses the most human of voices.

Once in your hands, the next thing is to get to know the geography of the violin. Imagine the violin as terrain. A violinist has to know their way around this terrain, and to do that you have to find routes and patterns of play across the four strings. You have to teach your fingers these routes, so that your fingers know the routes by heart. Your fingers have to become like London taxi drivers, so that when the call comes they know exactly how to get there and, equally important, how to get back. Instead of the grades came the virtuoso pieces, études, caprices, by violinist-composers such as Wieniawski, a Polish virtuoso of the 1800s who wrote his pieces primarily for himself, designed to show off his expertise and his lyrical skill. These are the vehicles through which you learn the geography of the violin, through which you master those routes. The pieces that you learn in these fierce, formative years are imprinted deep in the memory of your muscles. They are streets and alleyways and shortcuts. Your fingers will never forget.

If you listen closely to any of the great masters, you will hear how they each have different routes, make different patterns across the neck to find their way. Oistrakh, Kreisler, Heifetz: each takes their own itinerary, suiting their particular physique, their temperament, their violin. In this way is born the peculiar intimacy that is formed between a player and their violin, for it is of course part child that you are holding, part infant. How could it be otherwise, with its shape and the way it rests on your shoulders, close to your breast, close to your heart. Small wonder, then, that your violin behaves like an infant, capricious one day, sullen the next and then, for no obvious reason, sounds forth with songs of almost unbearable communication and overwhelming joy.

Yehudi Menuhin came to the school to give a master class. There were four of us. He wasn't performing by then but he spoke so eloquently that the music simply shone from within.

When my turn came I played Ravel's *Tzigane*, and he listened, and then, without warning, said, "Here! Let me show you!" He took my violin (one of only two times when I didn't mind), and started playing. His arm, his right arm, had gone by then, was very shaky, but he was Menuhin, and—oh my goodness—his tone, his feel! It was what I had been searching for. It wasn't that his playing wasn't intelligent, that it wasn't informed by thought, that he'd bypassed any cerebral process. It was simply that he'd gone straight for the artistic vision, in that small room, with that shaking arm. He'd aimed straight for it, and found it, dead center. And it came to me: this was what I needed for a mentor: a teacher who, like Menuhin, would be ruled by that vision, who saw music as something you plunge into, swim your way in and through. Music at the deep end.

Development, change, new horizons. Although I was still attending the Purcell Music School, I was now going twice weekly to the Royal College of Music. There I found a new teacher, one more suited to my outlook. His name was Felix Andrievsky.

Felix was a Russian with a big reputation, who, interestingly enough, had been brought over from the Soviet Union by Menuhin many years back. My mother had contacted him, asking for an audition. He hadn't any space in his class, but he promised that, if I came for an audition and was successful, his assistant might be able to take me on, and in a few years, if it worked out, maybe Felix himself (he didn't take children). I went with my mother. I was nine years old. We had to wait outside his office for his previous student to finish. He was wonderful right from the start, this busy bundle of energy bounding out of the room, very small. So I played, and afterward he said to my mother, "I've changed my mind. She is a little diamond and I want to be the one to polish her."

We took a taxi back home, my mother in a smiling good mood.

I started going to Felix initially once, then twice, a week. Jean came with me on my first half-dozen lessons or so. She felt it her duty to make the transition between teachers as positive an experience as possible. It was typical of such a wonderful teacher and woman. Felix's classroom was at the top of the Royal College, three flights of stairs, and a lift for the daunted. I liked walking up. There were toilets on the second and fourth floor. I always wash my hands before I start playing—it's part of my routine. (It's terribly disrespectful to play with dirty hands—over time the acid in your sweat will erode the varnish.) Before my class began, I'd put my violin down, rush to the second floor, run my hands under the water, dash back up. "Did you fly down?" he would joke, but the truth was, of course, I ran. I couldn't wait to get started.

Like the rest of the rooms in the college, it felt quite grand, gave you a sense of the privilege being accorded to you. His room became very familiar to me, somewhere where I belonged; the desk on one side of the room, the full-length mirror on the other (for the singers mainly, but for players to check their posture too). He always had with him a brown leather briefcase (never a violin case) in which lay records of all my lessons, what I had played. Felix was meticulous, very disciplined, but in a reassuring, anchored manner, rather than a repressed one. His life was an orderly one. A dead ringer for David Suchet's Hercule Poirot, five foot five, plump and fussy in his three-piece suit, he brimmed with an unquenchable vitality and a huge sense of fun. I felt safe, lucky to be with him. I was playing on my half-size when I started with him, and the first time he took it from me to show me something, I was amazed at how a man with such big fingers could produce such a beautiful sound from my undersized instrument. Felix opened my ears up to something I think I had known from the beginning: the importance of sounding good. (It's a debate that still rages: which is better, sounding good or saying something interesting?)

I never played scales with Felix, something that shocked my mother (for my mother scales were akin to learning your multiplication tables: something you simply had to master). I didn't learn a single scale with Felix. His philosophy was: it's all there in the music. You don't have to play the scales because you'll learn them through the music. He made me aware of the importance of reading between the notes. He was entertaining, full of encouragement, but he pushed me too, although it was only later that I became aware of how much. He was surprised by how quickly I could memorize pieces, asked me how I did it, imagining it was a photographic memory working on the score. But it wasn't that at all. It was my ear; that was all. Felix made my life fun, but he had his rules. He was originally from Ukraine, had studied in Moscow, then went to Israel. He was old-school Russian, full of the glory of the past, an incurable romantic. Although he was obsessive about his notation (the violin's fingering), there was another side to him which said that rules were made to be broken. I loved that idea, breaking walls down through the music. It was the music that mattered most to him. He was fascinating about Bach. Unlike most composers, Bach's manuscripts contain no dynamics, no notation at all. That,

Felix would say, was because Bach trusted his interpreters to have the intelligence to know what his intentions were. All you had to do was follow the authenticity of Bach's work.

His playing philosophy was exactly what I needed—all about freedom, interpretation, flexibility, and he took the idea of storytelling in one's music to another dimension. For a serious-minded child like myself, Felix was a breath of the freshest and most invigorating air, and at five o'clock every Tuesday and Friday, I would arrive at Room 72 ready to breathe it all in. It was an exciting time for both of us.

It was with Felix that I first appreciated the nature of a tutor's life, the pressure of rivalry that they exist under. When I was ten, another tutor came to give a master class. Felix told me to play, so I played. At the end, she said to him, "Well, I'd better get my prodigy out there first, then," and sure enough, a year later, the prodigy made her debut. It had never dawned on me before how much a teacher's success depends on the success of their students, but of course it's obvious. Students go to a teacher because of their reputation, and people only know if that teacher is any good once they've heard their students. That's how it works. When you're a child, the whole emphasis is on the future, whatever the strength of the spotlight. The question on everyone's lips is: "Is she going to fulfill her potential?" And so somewhere, deep down, you become wary of that future. It's lying in wait for you, like a dragon sleeping across the mouth of a cave, one eye shut, indifferent, one eye open straight on. The future could gobble you up alive. Mine and his.

There were hiccups. One time, in a lesson, the rosin began to do its dread work. I'd come to the lesson already breathless. The train had been late and my mother and I had hurried from the South Kensington tube station to the Royal College of Music. I started the lesson as normal, but very soon realized I was having an asthma attack. Breathing became hard, my eyes started watering. Even holding the violin became an effort. But these lessons were precious to me and very expensive (£70 an hour, an enormous sum in the 1990s). It came from a local-government grant, and my mother had been getting a lot of grief from the council over the cash—they were pushing for me to go to another, cheaper, teacher. She was having to fight them off, trying to maintain the best for me. So, there was a duty there for me to finish. I couldn't let my mother, my teacher, my school down. The need to complete this lesson was the imperative. Lessons were the most important thing in my life, the key to my future. I dug deep. My mother asked me if I was OK. I said yes, pretended everything was fine, gave it my best shot. And I got away with it. I finished the lesson, walked out.

But out on the street again my asthma reasserted itself. It wasn't going to let me get away that lightly. I collapsed on the pavement. Someone carried me to a phone box. I couldn't breathe, was turning blue. My mother, frantic, called an ambulance. It came, quite quickly, and they measured my lung capacity. Normal capacity is around three hundred liters per minute. I registered barely thirty. I'd hardly been breathing at all. Standing up, playing my heart out, my lungs had all but given up. So the matter of life and death and me and the violin became a literal thing; not simply of the soul, but of my body too. The violin would be my life, but the violin and its needs could be the death of me. Did we know it then, my mother and I, me collapsed in the street, my mother standing over me, saying, "Why didn't you tell me? Why didn't you say?" What did I have to say? What did she have to see? Was it then that I knew what was important to everyone, what was not—or was it just confirmation of what I'd suspected for a number of years? Didn't we understand this was how it was going to be for all of us?

Nevertheless, I felt cared for with Felix and as our lessons progressed and deepened, so did the bond between us. My earlier teachers had allowed me to develop in my own way, using whatever natural talent I had to find my own voice. Felix carried on this way of teaching but placed greater demands on me, higher expectations. It's what I thrived on. Encouragement, push, expectations. It helped me find my own driving spirit. He became a father figure, the man I looked up to, trusted, worked for. How could it have been otherwise?

Two years after we had come back to England, my grandfather came over to visit. We'd moved into the house that remained home until I spread my wings. It was an ex–council house on what was known as the Race Course Estate in Northolt. Every street was named after a British race course: Goodwood, Newmarket, and so on. The house had three bedrooms. My sister got the biggest (she always did), and I the smallest, the box room. I was very happy in my little room. It was my first sanctuary, a place I could get away to, get away from things.

Grandfather had named me, which means that I am named after him. His name was Ki-Jin. He took my sister's name, Min, and added his name, Jin. In Chinese lots of the same-sounding names use different characters. (In Korea you are taught Chinese characters. It's part of our tradition.) My character Min means people. Jin means fame. He was an old man by then, not frail but aged. By that point the whole family had realized that our departure had not been a temporary aberration, but that we were going to stay in England for good. Grandfather took this as an opportunity to travel overseas (something, other than going to Japan, he had never done). He was excited, bought a phrase book, learned little English sentences. He had never been to the West, yet he took a taxi from Heathrow to our home, put his bags down, took one look at the garden and said, "You need a lot of work on that." That's what he did, that July and August. He went out, found a place that sold him grass seeds, sowed them, planted lettuces, tomatoes, even strawberries—an old Korean man in an English garden, working the summer days away, something eternal within him, something of where he had come from, what he knew, the earth and the touch of it.

It was good to get to know him again, good for my mother too. She'd had a difficult time with him. Being a girl, being the youngest, she'd spent her formative years overlooked, taken for granted. She was bright, but as far as her parents were concerned, she needed to marry well. That was her destiny. Any interests she'd had weren't nurtured by them at all. So, with him over, it was an opportunity for him to see how she'd blossomed into a quietly confident woman—a woman who had brought her two children to this strange Western land and made a success of it, for them, and for her—she was a nursery school teacher by then. Grandfather stayed for the whole of the summer. One evening, the time for him to leave fast approaching, he asked me to play something for him. I didn't really want to. I was exhausted, having taken demanding classes all day. He said, "This might be the last time I hear you play."

I played the *Méditation*.

The night he left I sneaked back into my sister's room. While he'd been there I'd been sharing her room, and he'd slept in mine. I should have been happy to have my room back, but I wasn't. My grandfather had gone, and I knew I'd never see him again, knew something else too, that this feeling went beyond this one man, encompassed all of our long and complicated past (and future). We were a Korean family, but now we'd grow up never experiencing Korean life. We would grow up knowing things we couldn't know, the cousins we'd never meet, our uncles and aunts who would miss out on our lives, all abandoned for me and my violin. There was a hollow in us now, a hollow created by the violin and filled by the violin. The cause became the solace, though there were times when even the violin could not mask the hurt.

My half-size violin, the lovely Panormo, was exchanged, through the generosity of Charles Beare, who loaned me a three-quarter Gagliano. I met Charles for the first time, and even then, as a young Korean girl, was very struck by his English-gentleman ways. Charles is the stepson of William Beare (William being the son of Arthur Beare, half of the eponymous J. & A. Beare). J. & A. Beare have been at the forefront of instrument making and dealing for three generations, and Charles became its head in the 1960s. He is widely regarded throughout the world as *the* authority on authenticating and identifying instruments—his gift for spotting an instrument uncanny, his knowledge unsurpassed. He is one of the very few experts entrusted to repair and maintain violins belonging to such artists as Menuhin, Isaac Stern and Nathan Milstein.

I was sad to leave the Panormo, but I knew, when the time

came, I would be sadder to say goodbye to the Gagliano, for playing the Gagliano was the first time I felt the stirring of something stronger, of a love other than a familial love, rise within me for an object. It had, for a near-full-size, very slim shoulders, which fitted my body absolutely. Unlike its predecessors, which had been dark, the Gagliano had a marvelous amber hue that seemed to draw me into its depths, and from it came the sweetest sound I had yet heard within the cradle of my arms. This was the first instrument that sounded and had the appearance of a "grown-up" violin. Not surprisingly I wanted my response to be equally grown-up, and the thrill of unlocking its secrets was what I looked forward to every single day. There was no burden here, no thought of trial. To be apart from it was the trial. I looked after it as one might a baby, carefully cleaning the rosin from each string after every long practice, wrapping it in a silk scarf that had belonged to my mother before putting it to sleep every night. It became my closest friend, my closest companion. Often I would leave it out of its case between practice sessions, not because, as I told myself, it would be there to hand if an idea sprang into my mind, but because I needed it near me. It *was* me. Now I had to do it justice.

Prokofiev concertos, Paganini concertos, Mendelssohn: I began to run the gamut of the violin's play list, preparations all for the ultimate task ahead, the reality of public performance. They came too, one by one, a crescendo of expectations in themselves, each one with different demands, each one toughening me up, deepening my perspective, readying me for the moment when I would evolve from a gifted amateur into a professional. Money, of course, would be the final arbiter of that transition, and would bring with it a new set of demands, emotions and loyalties. But the trajectory was clear, the path seemingly cleared, step by step.

We met Peter Kiely, a sound engineer. He recorded music, but also did a lot of voice-overs, things like that. He had a studio in Neal Street, Covent Garden. I was playing a concert in Stanmore and he'd been hired to record it. He heard me playing and introduced himself, asked my mother and me if we'd like to come around to his studio, hear the result. I was about eleven then. He used to be a rock guitarist, realized he wasn't going to be the next Jimi Hendrix, so surrounded himself with tape. From that day on he recorded all my concerts, didn't charge anything, just brought his equipment around (equipment which would have cost thousands to hire) and set it all up. Now I could hear what I sounded like, get a feel for the balance. He had a fantastic ear. Later, it was through Peter that I would be introduced to Sir Georg Solti's wife. Peter invited a friend of his to come to a concert I gave, and he invited Lady Solti. She in turn asked her husband to come too. That is one of the good things about the classical music scene. There can be a camaraderie of excellence within it. Players talk about other players. Older players talk about younger players, give encouragement, make introductions. They know what it's like, and are happy to help. It's because of the music. Music demands appreciation, comment, engagement, reciprocation. In this way, it can be a generous art form, at one and the same time singular yet inclusive. A private performance in which discussion and expressions of appreciation are not allowed would be very hard to achieve. People *want* to talk about it, the people, the performance. That's what it's all about.

I'd been going along to my sister's piano lessons, where

we'd play Beethoven sonatas together. Her teacher was the wonderful dragon lady Maria Curcio, who had also taught the Argentinian pianist Martha Argerich. She had already taught me a technique which I have never forgotten, and which, if you look at a player's fingers (a violinist's, a pianist's) will go some way to explain the extraordinary speed with which we run up and down the board, race over those strings, those ivory keys. It's not simply about knowing where to go, or putting our digits down faster. It's about time. She told me that the faster you prepare your fingers to play, the slower your mind must feel. You have to feel as if you have all the time in the world. Hurry, and you will stumble. Take your time, and it's all there, stretching before you, the huge space of the fingerboard, your fingers poised and the notes just waiting to be shaped. If time gets the better of you, if you throw yourself at time's mercy, then time will take you down, but if you can see past time, let time elongate, then you can play it all.

Now she suggested that I play for Kyung Wha Chung. I traveled down to her house in Tunbridge Wells with my Gagliano and played. She invited me to play in a concert her brother was organizing back in Korea. I was growing out of the Gagliano and she arranged for me to borrow a 7/8 violin from, as ever, Charles Beare. I flew out to Korea with my mother; the first time I had gone back since we had left for England, those light years ago. I was there for three weeks and, though I saw my family, it was different this time. I was going to Korea to perform, not specifically to see them. My grandfather, who had spent time with us in London, who could perhaps have strengthened my connection with my Korean roots, had died. A couple of uncles came to the concert. My grandmother watched it on the television. No doubt there was a sense of vindication of my parents' decision—they could see the reason standing there on the stage—but it caused great friction in the family, my inability to fulfill the family obligations.

If you looked at my timetable for those three weeks you would understand why. I had back-to-back interviews from seven in the morning and then a concert in the evening. The only time I was able to meet them was after I'd played, and this caused some upset. To them it was as if I was disrespecting my family. I wasn't, there was no intention on my part to do such a thing, but that was the Korean reality, from which there should be no departure. Family *always* comes first, no matter what. A shift had come in perspective, theirs and ours. After the concert, we would be returning to England, to take further root in this alien world of violin and performance. They would remain in Seoul, living much as they had done, and always would, an ordered Korean life. I would grow up without all that. It would just be the four of us. And a violin.

And, as if acknowledging this change, my grandmother told my mother to back off regarding the Korean boy necessity. It was unfair and unrealistic to expect it. It wasn't going to happen, not as an edict. Both my mother and father had been determined to show the family that they were as Korean as they could be, but now Grandmother had given her permission to loosen the shackles. Don't put pressure on yourself to do this, she told my mother, because there isn't any pressure from here. We'd crossed over.

Traveling was beginning to be a part of my life: planes and trains, luggage and timetables, what to take, what to leave behind. At eleven I was nominated by the Purcell School for the Mozart International Competition in Bologna (the school sends out a tape recording of your work, and they either select you or they don't). The competition encompasses the whole range of musical instruments—wind, string, brass, percussion—and the hundred or so applicants are eventually whittled down to five. Out of these five comes the winner. Like many performers, I have an ambivalence about competitions. They are important, a way of making your mark, of jumping ahead—and, if you're a performer, taking center stage, wanting and being able to do these things are part of the deal. The competition was a prestigious one, the prize serious (£15,000), the finale televised.

We were in Italy for nearly a month, not just in Bologna but traveling around, giving concerts, promoting the competition, working up to the finale. There was a lot of hanging around, playing live on television without the luxury of warming up, so I learned how to warm up silently in my head, and to keep focused, the violin brain switched on, so when the time came I could play as I wanted to. Like all the other contestants I came with family or guardian, in my case my mother, and although it was a competition, we all mixed, perhaps because we weren't all playing the same instrument. We all became good friends over the few weeks on the competition tour, and I got on in particular with Victor, a charismatic percussionist and the firm favorite to win. He was talkative, good-humored and openly affectionate—I more reserved, but happy and comfortable in his company. It was fun chatting about the day's events.

One evening, after another long day and a performance on a TV show, we went to a park where we ran around, playing with leaves that had been swept into a heap—we were children, and life was full and amazing. Victor found a pinecone, a little one that hadn't fully opened yet, and put it in my hand. I looked at it and felt a real thrill. That night, I slept with the pinecone in my hand and, when I woke in the morning, it looked different. More open. Like me.

I didn't expect it, but I went through to be one of the five finalists. No chance of me winning, though. Everyone knew that it would be Victor. Competition day came. The culmination of everything we had been working so hard for these past few weeks. For the first time I felt a real tremor of doubt enter into my bones, not simply because of Victor's clearly demonstrable talent, but also because of the pieces that Felix had chosen for me to play—Brahms's *Sonatensatz*, a Bartók Rhapsody and Paganini's Caprice No. 16. Paganini's caprices are fiendishly difficult. It's said that his very appearance, his gaunt features, his funereal clothing, his sloping shoulders gave him a satanic edge. It wasn't his clothing that drew the crowds, though, it was his extraordinary playing, itself something that many people thought not quite of this world. When he went to Vienna in the spring of 1898 the town responded with a sort of collective hysteria. "The most wonderful, extraordinary musical phenomenon, a comet on the musical horizon, a kind of which returns perhaps once in a thousand years, is at this time within our walls," the Dresden *Abendzeitung* wrote. Paganini became the talk of the town, as he became the talk of Europe. And his dress too became a thing of fashion—boots, gloves, hats, all were sold "à la Paganini." Schubert, who went to see his second, and possibly his first, concert there, bought tickets for his fourth and told his friend Eduard von Bauernfeld, "I tell you, we shall never see this fellow's like again."

The caprice I had to play, No. 16, lives up to its reputation,

((♪3))

a piece designed to tie you up in knots, testing you to see if you have the wit to unravel the puzzle. On the surface it's a series of wild arpeggios, peaks and troughs rising and falling with astonishing rapidity. It's a white-water-rafting piece, and to navigate it at all is a feat of endurance. To do so with panache, to give this ride form, is another thing altogether. I rang Felix back in England, voicing my doubts. He did what any good coach does: he sweet-talked me; he strengthened my resolve; he ordered me back in. So it went: the Brahms, the Bartók, the Paganini. I started playing, and for some reason everything seemed to align—like ducks in a row, I could just move my fingers, hit the target. Everything was clear. Everything was open. I had nothing to lose, just wanted to play well and feel free. It was all there in front of me. I forgot how tiring the last few weeks had been and just played. When I'd finished, I looked at the judges. They looked back at me. One of them smiled.

We waited for the results. A tall, beautiful woman began speaking Italian, which I didn't understand—and then: "Victor," she announced. The audience clapped and cheered. Ah, Victor has won, I said to myself. I felt disappointment that I hadn't won but also a glow inside for my friend. He deserved it. My violin was still in my hands, ready to play again, just in case. The winner was to give a repeat performance to see the program out. Now, my hands relaxed. I let my mind rest, change from violin mode to just being a girl of eleven again. I smiled as Victor accepted his trophy, cheered him on with the others. But then the presenter made another speech, and gave another name: "Maria." Again, the audience clapped as Maria, a pianist, went to collect her trophy. Confused, I looked around, not understanding what was happening, lost. Then suddenly I heard my name. The woman smiled, beckoned toward me. I got up and walked onto the stage, still feeling strange.

"Play Paganini," she said.

"What? Me? Paganini? Now?"

She laughed and gave me a hug. "Yes, Paganini."

They had announced the prizes in reverse order. I had won. And so I played, in a daze, the violin brain barely engaged. Paganini, I am afraid, suffered accordingly. And the £15,000? That was set aside, for when I would truly move from one world into the next. It went toward the time when I would buy my first serious, grown-up, soloist-worthy violin.

It was not only the quality of my violin tuition that contributed to me winning that competition. The quality of the school I attended, the Purcell School, had also played its part. While Felix demanded and extracted every ounce of ability from me as a player, the school broadened my musical horizons: choir, music theory, music history. I was beginning to play almost everything I could—Mendelssohn, Prokofiev, and so on—though there were two concertos that I did not try, the Beethoven and the Brahms. There was a logic behind not learning them yet—rather in the same vein as an actor might delay playing Hamlet . . . I wasn't quite ready for them. I hadn't the depth or the violin to begin to do them justice. I would listen to them though. I was listening too to other violinists, beginning to appreciate the what and the how they brought to the music.

Not long after winning the prize I flew to Zürich, my first proper paid gig, £1,000. It was with a youth orchestra at the Tonhalle: two matinees played back to back, and I was to play Mozart's Concerto No. 2 and Sarasate's *Zigeunerweisen*.

Felix had been approached by the organizers to find a young violinist who could play the demanding (or, as he preferred to say, the technically sophisticated) *Zigeunerweisen*, and he put me forward. As I learned the Mozart concerto, Felix told me that the reason this concerto was not the best example of Mozart's genius was because Mozart had become enamored of the new fortepiano and had begged his father to buy him one. His father, Leopold, bargained with him that if he wrote five violin concertos, the fortepiano would be his. How true this story is I still don't know, but it was a good one to stoke the imagination. Like many concertos, this one contains a cadenza, the open space in the music where the soloist is offered the chance to showcase his or her abilities—both in skill and imagination—and in the past, it was not unusual for the soloist to improvise. Cadenzas are a mixed blessing. It's a time when the body of the orchestra falls silent, the conductor rests his baton. It's your time and your time alone. From the nineteenth century, it became customary for composers to write a cadenza for the soloist in the score. But, before that, it was more irregular—some Mozart concertos have a cadenza written by the composer, but not all. It's the same with Beethoven. There are violinists such as Kreisler who have written such brilliant cadenzas that it's not only difficult for other violinists to do anything other than follow in their footsteps; more than that, it is a joy to do so. Kreisler's Beethoven cadenza is such a one. I once managed to give myself an asthma attack while attempting to compose a song, singing my lungs out into my mother's new hi-fi recording microphone—not something that came effortlessly to me. But I got through the task of composing my own cadenza for this Mozart concerto. To my ears it was obviously a child's composition, but I still remember every note. And in recent years I have developed the original version and still play it in concert.

⌒

A friend played me Ginette Neveu. She was intriguing from the very start, a child prodigy, her concert debut at seven, achieving worldwide celebrity at the age of fifteen when, in competition with the older David Oistrakh and a hundred and eighty others, she won the International Henryk Wieniawski Violin Competition in 1934 (the same Wieniawski who'd given us all those show pieces to hone our technique). The perfection of her playing dazzled everyone who heard it. Her tutor Carl Flesch once told her, "My child, heaven has bestowed upon you a gift, and I do not intend to interfere." She was a refreshingly singular figure, fond of sports, pedaling around the streets of Paris in her big boots and bare legs, her violin case hanging from the handlebars. As her fame grew she toured extensively with her brother, a pianist, and though the Second World War had partly suspended her career, she resumed her globe-trotting path soon afterward.

In October 1949, a few days after giving a concert in Edinburgh—where she played one of her own showpieces, Ravel's *Tzigane*—she died, along with everyone else, when her plane crashed into a mountainside after a stopover at São Miguel in the Azores, on its way to America. She was found in the wreckage, her precious Stradivarius still gripped in her hand. Apocryphal? You read it in some sleeve notes, you don't in others. The world is probably divided into two types of people—those who don't play the violin who think the story over-fanciful, and those who play the violin who can envisage exactly how that would happen.

If this story, resonant with the tragic love for her instrument, her complete commitment to her world, an abandonment to music's fate, hadn't captivated me, her playing would. Listen to her now if you can. She carries an extraordinary intensity, totally unlike the violinists of today, the bow unrestrained, unashamed, and in the execution a kind of nakedness that is unlike any other violin player I have ever known. Edith Piaf's lover, the boxer Marcel Cerdan (who was also on the plane), was reputed to have said that he would travel the length of the earth to hear Neveu play, and if you listen to her rendition of the Brahms concerto you will understand why. Even with the limitations of a 1949 recording, it's an experience, a jolt to the senses. No wonder she held on to her Stradivarius in those last few minutes. It would have been as essential to her life as her very breath.

It was getting closer, my time as a young girl shortening quickly. I was growing, in every sense. My first truly professional event came unexpectedly. A previous pupil of Felix's had come back to visit him and had sat in on one of my lessons. Her husband, Gonzalo Augusto, was a Spanish impresario and after hearing me she was emboldened enough to speak to him. A phone call later to my mother, and it had been arranged. I was to play a recital at the Serenates d'Estiu festival in Majorca. This was a big trial for a twelve-year-old. This was no competition for juniors, no friendly concert where concessions are made for age. This was serious. Two weeks of top-flight concerts, a host of world-famous musicians. The moment had come.

I had the whole of June to practice—five brand-new pieces, including Saint-Saëns, Introduction and *Rondo Capriccioso*. ((♪4)) Felix gave me daily lessons at home, incredibly intense, lots of tears, lots of frustration, the pressure never dropping, the understanding with all of us, Felix, my mother, my sister, myself, that this was what we had all been working toward. There could be no turning back. Day after day, hour after hour, the work relentless. We arrived a week early, the hotel overlooking a gloriously sunny beach and the most tempting of seas. Felix swam as often as he could, my mother occasionally, but I wasn't allowed anywhere near the water. It would break my focus, and focus, concentration, was paramount. As for all my other performances, Felix had chosen what I would play. We'd practice in the morning, I would have a siesta in the afternoon, then we'd practice some more.

He started the ritual of giving me a glass of lemon and honey before playing—lemon to focus the mind, honey to give me energy—a ritual which stays with me to this day. My diet was similarly controlled—no fatty *jamón*. Fat makes you dehydrate, lose concentration. I already knew how important diet was—how a heavy, sluggish meal would often bring out a heavy and sluggish performance—and a lot of the girls at school were obsessed about their weight. Diet was simply another element of my career, being a performer, how I looked, the impression I gave (young, pretty, feminine, but not adult), no less important than applying rosin to my bow, or running through scales four hours a day. It was all part of the same thing, part of the whole, the experience of playing the violin. The totality of what playing demanded was expanding, dictating every aspect of my life.

The d'Estiu festival was a huge deal. After that, everything took off. I got my first professional fee for this performance. Gonzalo signed me up: he found me work; serious playing, serious money, money I put aside for the day I would buy my own violin. I started doing five or six concerts a year, mainly in Spain and Italy: Madrid, Seville, Bologna. It was the beginning of my orchestrated life or, if it went badly, the possible end to it. Only it wasn't going to go badly. Why should it? I was a child prodigy. Triumphant accomplishment was bred into my bones.

And then it went completely wrong, the edifice of success, of who I was, what I was going to be. Cracking first under one strain, then another. I was just a few months from fourteen. Felix wanted me to go on holiday with him, to Gstaad. Putting it down in words like that makes it sound extraordinary (on holiday with your tutor!), and of course it was, but he was my mentor, and I, along with everyone else, was in thrall to him. I wasn't going with him alone. There would be another student going, her mother too. But it did demonstrate who called the shots here, who was in charge. My mother might have been nervous—I was still only thirteen—but she acquiesced. She would fly out a few days later. Felix ran my life now, decided what I should play, what I should eat, what was good for me. Off we went on holiday, Felix behind the wheel.

We drove, two long days, in his big Mercedes (he was very proud of his car), me in the back, stopping over in France for the night. It was a long, boring journey, a full day's driving the first day, a full day's driving the next. I'd been seasick crossing the Channel, the first time I'd ever been on a ferry, and by the time we got to Gstaad we were all tired. We were staying in chalets. Felix's apartment was above mine. We unpacked. I'd brought my ghetto blaster. There's not a lot to do in Gstaad apart from skiing or going out to eat. Felix wanted to go to the cinema, so we piled back in the car. I remember talking about what we were going to eat while staying there. I was leaning forward, not wearing a seat belt, the conversation centering on the delights of Russian soup. Next instant and I was doing that thing that seems like lazy writing—I was seeing stars. Unbelievable, jagged, wrenching pain and seeing stars. Felix had had an accident with an oncoming car. Ever since I could walk I'd been trained by my mother not to cry if I fell over, and besides, I was thirteen, far too old to indulge in all that nonsense, but suddenly I was aware of someone screaming. Screaming and screaming. It took me a moment to realize it was me.

The screaming stopped. A passerby came to my rescue. That was fortunate, as they told us there was a doctor who lived in a house across the road. We knocked on his door. He examined me, said there was a possibility of a concussion, thought I should go to hospital, talked as if I weren't there. Perhaps I wasn't quite. Felix didn't seem to like that idea. I was asked if I had travel insurance. Luckily, I did, but as I'd just thrown up, the doctor insisted anyway, insurance or no. I don't remember getting there, only the kindness of the doctors once in intensive care. I did have a concussion, but it was my face that brought me the pain. Felix and the rest were unharmed, but I had fractured my cheekbone.

Now came a bizarre dance, acted out by Felix, the other student's mother, the doctors and me. The hospital wanted to keep me in overnight. I was lonely, frightened, wanted to call my mother. We had arranged that I would call her every evening, just to let her know how things were going. The others weren't keen on the idea. There was this madness circling around my bed: Felix and the other student's mother on one hand, on the other the doctors standing in their white coats, saying, "Doesn't she need to call home?" Eventually they re-lented. A phone was brought in. I was allowed to speak to her. I tried my best to tell her that everything was fine, but my voice must have told her something was up. She started quiz-zing me. I had to hang up.

Back at home, she grew worried. She tried to call the cha-lets where we were staying but, naturally, there was no an-swer from my room. The following day there was no answer either. So the next time I called her, the next evening as I was supposed to, she wore me down, got the truth out of me. She flew out straight away.

Here's where you expect sparks to fly: an incensed mother, a defensive tutor. But the combination of a Korean mother and a Russian teacher doesn't have the required combustible materials on hand. In Korea it's instilled in you to have the utmost respect for your professor; challenging their position is most certainly not part of the deal. The Soviet school is very much "I am the teacher. I am the expert. Do not question my authority." Even though my mother was seething, she could only express her anger to me. Even when she did promise to have it out with Felix, I would beg her not to.

Enough said. He didn't mean for it to happen, and I don't think he saw the full measure of what he'd done, what he expected of me, who he imagined I ultimately answered to. But it was the beginning of the end of our relationship. Though everyone around me was furious, initially my loyalty to him kicked in and I stayed. He was my teacher, my guide. He knew me like no one else. I needed him. It was just an unfortunate accident, that was all. But, of course, though I didn't quite see it then, the trip was not about a holiday. It was about possession.

My father returned. He'd been waiting for Daewoo to post him back to England. Mum was very good friends with the wife of the CEO and she'd promised that she'd help engineer Dad's return, but the CEO had died unexpectedly and the opportunity had died with him. The alternatives were uncertain. He could stay in Libya, but he didn't want that. He wanted to be part of a family again. He thought about driving a taxi here, but Mum was against it. He didn't *have* to do anything. I was starting to earn good money: £1,000 a concert at first, rising to £3,000. That was a proper salary, plus I had the competition winnings. So my violin could give them a semblance of security and stability. They made the decision. My father took the leap of faith, packed his bags, came home. He didn't work for a whole year, while he set up his new construction business—a year of real uncertainty. It was never talked about—too humiliating, I think, for both of them, and I was a bit indignant about that, a bit brattish, thought that they'd just taken my money, didn't trust them to do the right thing, look after me, *my* interests.

It wasn't the only problem. Money aside, his absence meant that he hadn't been a close part of my sister's and my growing up. We were children of a highly traditional marriage, at least in the beginning. My father earned the money. Children were a mother's territory. Even when he was living with us, I barely saw him. I don't think, when we were kids, he knew what to do. He'd work and go out and play golf with his colleagues. One time my mother cajoled him, telling him that he should get to know his children better, take them out for the day. I was quite excited at the prospect, imagining all sorts of delights. He took us to the driving range; we watched him tee off. But that wasn't his fault. He was a Korean father. Suddenly he was back in the household, quite a stranger to my sister and me. I was a teenager now, not the eight-year-old he'd lived with last time around. A treat for him was buying me an ice cream (still is). He found it difficult to adjust. He was trying to keep the family bound together in the traditional Korean way, but instead had these three women under his roof who were flying out in all directions. I was making a success of the violin, my sister was excelling on the piano and by this time my mother had qualified as a teacher in a nursery school. And more than this. In my world, I had teachers who I was close to, closer than I was to him. I had relationships with them, ones that ran into the very core of my being, ones of creativity and voice, ones of learning and desire— ones that he had been excluded from, and that he could never fully enter. We were all, in our own way, independent. Our course had been set and we'd followed it—were following it—without him. And now he was with us. He didn't know what his role was anymore. He had no connection to this England now he was here, living off his teenage daughter. That must have been hard for him, something that would have gone against everything he had been taught. What is extraordinary about him, what I admire most in him, is how flexible, how relaxed, how positive about a woman's right to the world she wants, he has become, and, considering where he came from, what he knew, what he'd been taught to believe, how little time it took him.

Understandably he didn't take to Felix. Part of it was a father trying to reestablish contact with his daughter— territorial. But principally it sprang from an understanding of Felix's perception of me, his expectations. Felix had begun to take ownership of my career. He wouldn't let me play to anybody without his say-so. What had started off as an almost magical relationship was turning into something driven by money, power and success. (The accident still bore its scars, some of them physical. Every now and again he'd touch my cheek, say, "Hasn't that healed yet?" It hadn't.) All the traits that had endeared him to me became overwhelming, suffocating. I felt that he had become more and more possessive, jealous of anybody else in my life. Others commented on how he'd talk about me in my presence as if I weren't there, how he'd follow me around, dog my footsteps.

There was a pivotal day at school. I was recording the Sibelius concerto. Peter was there with his equipment, a pianist called Gordon Back, who used to come to my lessons once a week, play whatever I needed. Felix just wouldn't leave me alone. I'd tell him I needed to take five minutes out, and he'd come with me, wouldn't let me be by myself. Exasperated, I said to Gordon, "Is this normal?" Gordon thought it most definitely was not. "He should back off," he said.

I started rebelling. Felix had set this task for me—to memorize a new piece every week. Every week I had to come into the room and play a new concerto movement that I had learned by heart. It sat there like a balance on scales; his demand and my compliance. But I didn't want that balance anymore. That balance no longer seemed right. So I stopped, or rather I'd learn them secretly (because I wanted to learn them, I needed to) but I wouldn't show him. I'd turn my life away from him. It sounds obtuse, bloody-minded, but for me it was a way of weakening his hold, slackening the rope. I found another way too—a little more extreme, a little more obviously confrontational. He had a real thing about fingering. I was only allowed to follow his notation, only allowed to read from photocopies of his marked-up music, none other permitted in my possession. I did it his way or I didn't do it at all.

Maybe it would have stayed that way a little longer, but I went to see Anne-Sophie Mutter play. She was in mesmerizing form, but what transfixed me was not just her extraordinary stage presence, but her fingering: nothing like mine, yet so natural, so expressive, so obviously *her*. Something inside me snapped. I decided I should try to find my own way. It was like a shaft of light, breaking through the cloud. *My own way.* I started watching videos of other players, soaking in all the different fingerings that seemed to fill the screen: so many different approaches, so many different players, so many different interpretations. I'd untied a knot, but now I felt constrained physically. My fingers, my route. I took a saw to that rope and with my own fingering started down my own path. I'd make a lot of mistakes. Looking back, I can see that I went wrong many, many times, played an open note when it would have been more appropriate on another string, but they were *my* mistakes, *my* way of searching. It was my right, my basic, almost human right to choose. Who I was, and who I was going to be had been kept from me without me really noticing. Perhaps this is what all teenagers feel, a sense of self trying to break free, but there was something so tangible in this. And it was the violin that was my route out, a violin with a body and a neck and a yellow brick road of a fingerboard.

My fingers started to be themselves. It's a strange thing to write now—that sense of freedom they began to tap out.

There was more. The outside world was breaking in and there was nothing anyone could do to stop it. My GCSEs were coming up. Felix wasn't interested in that. GCSEs meant more homework, not so much time for practice. I was a violinist. The rest didn't really matter. But it did to me. I was young but I'd always had the fear of becoming an uneducated musician, of not knowing the depths of what I might be playing. Playing isn't simply the notes, it's what you can bring to it, not simply your ability, but your intelligence, musical and otherwise. I don't know how true it was, but playing that time back in Korea, I'd picked up an attitude that if you were a musician, it meant that you were a little slow, a little dim-witted, that all you could do was play; not think, or talk, or know, but play. I didn't want to be that type of musician. Doing well at school, getting good grades, became of paramount importance to me, very much at odds with the training and Felix's vision—and also the vision I once thought I had of myself. That vision was starting to fog up too, or rather one day the fog lifted, and I saw something else.

I was sitting on a train, violin case at my feet, watching a bunch of schoolchildren in uniform giggling away, not a care in the world. Fifteen-year-olds like me. If they had any cares, they were teenage cares, ones they could share. A note sounded in me—no, more than a note, a whole chord of regret sweeping me up. Of course, this wasn't exactly a new feeling. I knew what I was seeing—a normality that was denied me. But this time it was as if I were standing apart, looking at a Min who wasn't there, who couldn't be there, who had never joined in, never would. And I'd never felt that before, never understood the totality of what had happened to me, never quite grasped that sense of exclusion that had been imposed upon me, watching these young girls who I had never met. And it came to me that, in a parallel world, I should be there, alongside *my* friends, sharing *my* jokes, *my* worries. But I'd never had that. When any of my friends had held birthday parties, though I'd get invited, it had always been assumed I wouldn't be free to go. I'd be practicing or learning a new piece. I hadn't time for frivolities like parties. I had serious things to do. When they went on a school trip, I didn't go with them. I'd have a new work to prepare, a concert to give, and later, when they laughed and joked about the great time they'd all had, I could only listen, unable to join in. Sure, I did my share of traveling abroad, did things they didn't, couldn't, but I did them with a teacher or a parent in tow, with an adult but all the while alone. My school friends were like family to each other while I was always set apart. Who else was there for me but my violin?

And quite suddenly I didn't want to step out onto the stage anymore, no longer the performing puppet. I'd come back to it (perhaps) when I was older, and would do a few in-house concerts to keep my hand (my fingers) in shape. As for the rest, I would start to have a life, inhabit the world my friends lived in, no longer looking at it through the study window, but with my head and heart planted firmly within it. I was a teenager! I hadn't had a childhood. My childhood had been eaten away, and now the friends I'd had since the age of eight were moving on to different stages of their lives, while I seemed to be on the same track, moving yet not moving; Min the violinist getting ahead every day, every week, but Min the person going nowhere. Starting a career when you're as young as I was does peculiar things to you, things that don't really become apparent until you're a little older. You're exposed to the ways of the adult world and, while you have the capacity to understand it, it doesn't sit well on you. Your life has been accelerated and you've been driven past a whole chunk of it at breakneck speed. There it goes! Your childhood! Gone! Never to come back! One moment you were a child living with your parents, the next you're out there on stage, violin in hand and concertos in your head and no in between.

I just broke. No more. The little diamond was tired of being taken out and polished. She had to leave.

It was done badly, abruptly, just as I was auditioning for the Royal College of Music. I wrote Felix a Dear John letter. He was devastated. "I've given my life to you," he said, "and you've left me with nothing." He tried to make contact, but every time I ghosted him. Immature, unkind, a little heartless, I was all those things, but also a little confused. There didn't seem to be any other way.

Don't get me wrong. I didn't want to abandon the violin, but I wanted to be an equal partner to it, wanted how I played and when I played to be my decision, mine and my violin's. I needed a teacher still, but a different type of teacher. I'd become a variable player. I had good days and I had bad days. But if you want to be a classical performer on the stage you need to become like a top-flight tennis player. Your ability has to be at a certain level—all the time. You need that second serve. That's what I needed. I needed to be able to play so that on a good day I could fly, but whatever the circumstances there'd always be a certain level below which I'd never fall. And that's what another Russian, Grigori Zhislin, taught me. Grigori proved to be the toughest teacher yet.

Zhislin couldn't have been more different. Whereas Felix had been all about interpretation, Zhislin was the exact opposite. Felix wasn't interested in the rules. For Zhislin, life didn't exist outside them. He was absolute Soviet-school textbook. You played his way, or you didn't play at all. As I've said, Felix hadn't cared a fig about scales. For Zhislin, they were Stations of the Cross. That was just the beginning. There were hard and fast procedures for everything. If I didn't vibrate exactly seven and a half times on a note, all hell would break loose. Lesson time was a moveable feast. I was supposed to have my weekly session with him at ten o'clock, but often it didn't work out that way. He'd oversleep, or forget, get someone to leave a message in my pigeonhole: "Sorry. Come to my house in a couple of hours." No mobile phones then, you understand, and I'd have bused in all the way to college to get there on time. Back in his own country, Russia, he'd been a huge star, winner of any number of competitions, but when he came over to England, he thought nobody recognized his true worth. The glittering international career he'd counted on never materialized. He was reduced to teaching.

This was the trouble. He was a great artist with no place to go. Everyone who heard him recognized his worth (students flocked to him), but the unhappiness with the world he found himself in took its toll. He was a heavy drinker.

He had his problems too. He'd chain-smoke throughout the lesson (something that didn't do my asthma any good), often smelling of drink. Though he could be the most charming man in the room, he had a temper. He would take my bowing arm, fling it back and forth. "No! Not like that! Like this!" Going to Zhislin, coming back from Zhislin, took its toll. My mother would say, "Ignore the bad stuff, just take what's good," but that was easier said than done. He wasn't a natural. He'd pick on everything I did. One time when I was in a master class with him, playing the Sibelius concerto, he would let me play only a single note. "Why are you playing like that?" he demanded. "It should be like this!"

I thought about Felix. The truth was I missed him. And feeling lost in this new strange relationship with Zhislin, remembering Jean's kindly guidance when I joined Felix's class, I decided—in retrospect, perhaps naively—to go along to a master class Felix was giving in Lübeck to seek his counsel, his advice. Even his presence, I imagined, would do something for me. I'd known him so well. It didn't go as planned. I was seventeen years old, on the cusp of adulthood, no longer the teenager in the midst of puberty he had last seen. The meeting was awkward, felt forced and I felt unwelcome. I don't blame Felix for this. It must have been strange for him too. One evening, as was the tradition in his class, they all went to a restaurant with Felix and his wife and I was invited to go along by the other students. I hesitated, as it was clear by this point that the reunion was a bit of a disaster, but I was cajoled into going. Felix sat in the midst of his class in stony silence, resolutely ignoring me, even if I tried to talk with him. His wife, whom I had adored in the good old days, was clearly embarrassed and felt a bit sorry for me. She said, "Come on, Fell" (her name for him), "Min asked you a question." No response. I felt terribly sad. After all we had gone through, it seemed a shame to end like this. He'd been so good for me, despite the outcome I flew back to London knowing that the door to any further relationship with Felix was firmly shut. It was back to Zhislin, like it or not.

He sounds impossible, and in many ways he was, but he also had a lot to offer. A huge Heifetz fanatic, he admired that steely brilliance, and during those teenage years I shared his adoration. Heifetz represented to me everything the perfect violinist could be. I was an unashamed geek of a fan, seeking out fellow Heifetz fanatics at the Purcell School and the

RCM, sharing favorite records. (I think I have pretty much everything he ever played on tape.) In the sleeve notes for Heifetz's 1959 recording for RCA of both Mendelssohn's and Prokofiev's concertos, the violinist Joseph Wechsberg remembers one afternoon in Beverly Hills when he asked Heifetz how he'd played a hugely difficult passage in a concerto (sadly he doesn't say which) that had outfoxed him and many other violinists. Apparently, Heifetz shrugged his shoulders, picked up his violin (a Guarneri) and played it there and then, but at such a speed that Wechsberg was unable to discover how he'd done it. He asked Heifetz if he'd do it again, which Heifetz duly did, but still Wechsberg wrote, "I hadn't the faintest idea how he'd done it. Seeing the blank look on my face, he shook his head sadly at such ignorance."

Heifetz, of course, was another prodigy—performing the Mendelssohn concerto at seven years old on a half-sized violin in prerevolutionary Russia to an audience of a spellbound thousand, who marveled at the way his tiny fingers conquered the intricacies of the last movement. Heifetz's overwhelming art is easy to oversimplify. His mastery, his "cold tonal beauty," as it has been described, is as awesome as it's possible to be. In most live performances a professional solo violinist at the top of their game might make four or five minor errors. Heifetz would be unlikely to make one, such was his control. Not surprisingly I admired his cool demeanor, which, to his critics, was an indication of his aloofness—an interpretation I felt passionately indignant about. I saw it for what it was, a sign of an impeccably, impossibly disciplined artist with complete dedication to his craft. To me, Heifetz was like the proverbial swan, gliding effortlessly across the pond while paddling furiously underneath. Listen beyond the dazzlingly brilliant technique, the breakneck tempo and you hear the potent mix of his almost eerie beauty and burning fire. But it was Heifetz's textbook virtuosity that Zhislin demanded— competition-winning stuff. There was nothing natural about Zhislin. Unsurprisingly, we fought a lot.

But if you stood up to him . . . One day Zhislin rang up my house. Lesson delayed. This time he needed an emergency appointment with the dentist. Could we take him? Of course we could. My mother was allowed to drive now (yes, times did change) and we waited an hour and a half for him to get his teeth fixed. Afterward, it was time for my lesson, but dental work had put him in an even filthier temper than usual. On it came, the old routine, shouts and yells: Do this, do that, didn't I understand *anything*? And my mother, standing amid the barracking for the first time, appalled, said, "Don't do that, please. Don't yell at my daughter." Zhislin shriveled up. He just shrank back, reduced in size and vigor. And funnily enough, after that, I no longer respected him. He wasn't who I thought he was. It was coming to a close.

We're working toward the time now, the time I met my violin. Five years to go. I went about being a student at the Royal College of Music. I set about getting my degree. I went through a succession of violins. I had fun, burned the two-ended candle. I was younger than everyone else (sixteen), but I kept that quiet. I could be irresponsible if I liked. Or not. It was my choice. I had my classes, I had my in-house concerts, I maintained my stubborn streak. I didn't have a manager anymore but I hadn't given up, and in truth I didn't want to. The whole point of being at the Royal College was to prepare you to be a professional musician, and I was happy to hunker down. At the end of the year, when I was seventeen, my practical-skills teacher arranged my debut at St. John's Square, in the heart of London. It was within the college sphere, so that was all right with me. With that concert came my first opportunity to play a Stradivarius. My teacher started booking me for other concerts. I started performing again, but I had more control this time. It wasn't made out to be such a big deal. The door had never really closed, I'd just pushed it shut for a while. In my second year a concert I played was broadcast on Radio 3. In the rehearsal I'd met Georg Solti and he'd liked what he'd heard. Afterward Lady Solti got in touch with my parents and arranged for me to go to his house to meet him again but, sadly, that was not to be. He died a month later.

It might have gone on like that for quite a while, me dipping my toes in now and then, playing this and that—who knows? When I'm asked, how did I get back into it, the high-octane stuff, the answer comes quickly and simply. I fell in love like only a nineteen-year-old girl can—and with the wrong person.

His name was Robert. I'd never had a boyfriend before, almost a deliberate choice on my part. My sister's first relationship when a teenager had caused no end of trouble within the family, mixed-up boyfriend, mixed-up family reactions, blame heaped on everyone night and day, and I wanted no part of it. And there was the Korean thing too. We weren't expected to have any relationship before that idealized Korean boy popped over the horizon. Those were the rules. But love doesn't wait for Korean Mr. Right, or care about what your parents want. It's indiscriminate, dangerous, can come out of nowhere and, if you're unlucky, can lead to much the same place.

He was five years older, and a lot more experienced. Robert seemed to offer me something I had never imagined before, a life outside the violin. He wasn't interested in the violin. He was interested in me. He wanted me to be an ordinary girl, a girl-next-door, told me as much. He even asked me whether I could consider a life without the violin. In my imagination I could just about picture it, this alternative, unknown world, hardly conceivable before I met him. But I thought about it then. For a short time all my concerns seemed to disappear. I was in love and it was fabulous. It was as if I'd grown up over-night, had gone to sleep Min the ex–child prodigy dreaming of her violin, and woken up Min an ardent young woman thinking of her man. It hit me like a freight train. I'd had male friends, but never attached any kind of romantic notion to them. It came all at once, overwhelmed me. And I couldn't imagine how life could go on without it.

Life quickly taught me that it could. I soon realized that Robert's indifference to the violin wasn't indifference at all, but something a good deal more serious. His distrust of the violin was all-consuming. His father was a highly successful musician, the life and soul of the party. Robert was a musician too, and a talented one, but the shadow of his father loomed large. Shy, introverted, he felt he could never match up to his father's showy gifts, brooded on it, on what music had done to them all. My violin was a reminder of it. Robert resented it, was quite open about it, admitted to the rising jealousy he felt whenever considering its hold on me. The girl he thought he could turn me into had a rival suitor, and he simply couldn't cope. My life was too unstable. He wanted someone who was standard, average, routine, someone who came with nothing attached.

It was a mayfly love, brilliant, glorious, flights of sun-lit wonder, and over before it had barely started. Broken-hearted, I wrote my mum a letter, putting down all my feelings. I wrote it in the same headlong rush as the affair it-self, the emotions welling up inside me, how this love of mine had filled me with hopes and feelings and desires that had entered my body like a fever, and now that it had gone, left me weak, bereft, incapable. I told her I didn't know how I was ever going to recover from it, couldn't see a way out, two pages of utter despair, two pages begging for help. I gave it to her and she sat there, read half of it, and said, "What's the matter? Are you drunk?"

We never talked about it again.

So I found the way out myself. I became angry with the idea of him, angry that he should have tried to cut me off from the thing that defined me. Like that day in the schoolgirl-filled railway carriage, it came to me like a shot. That's who I am. I'm not going to cut that side of me off as if it were an illness. It wasn't an illness. It was the healthiest, most alive part of me. I became determined to reignite my musical life.

I bought my first violin, a Carlo Bergonzi, a gorgeous Ital-ian instrument, bought it with the competition and concert money that my parents had invested for me. They hadn't spent my money, merely borrowed it, then put it to work on my behalf. I bought it for about a quarter of a million pounds, bought it, luckily, just before the prices for Bergonzis boomed. I left Zhislin. Outside the college I'd found a new tutor, the legendary Ruggiero Ricci, based at the Mozarteum University of Salzburg.

Ruggiero Ricci was an Italian-American, born Roger Rich. His immigrant father anglicized their family name when he arrived in America, but Ruggiero himself changed his name back as a conscious re-adoption of his Italian roots. He was right to do it. He had an Italian, extrovert flair to him, and with his natural virtuosity it is no surprise that it was Ricci who mastered Paganini's caprices and brought them to a new life. The first violinist to record them all in their original, astonishing format, he revealed them to be not simply mind-boggling exercise pieces, but something else, something of a complex and fierce poetic, hard to follow at times, but worth the effort. He saw the thread in them and followed it through. He had been a prodigy, like me, but his star had risen at greater speed, giving his breathtaking debut in San Francisco at the age of ten, and his first appearance at New York's Carnegie Hall the following year, 1929. He had been invited to play in front of Kreisler, who, afterward, had lifted him in his arms and told him, "Always play as you feel." (Ginette Neveu had expressed the same sentiment, only differently: "The most important thing for an artist is her individuality and that must continue to grow.")

I phoned Ricci soon after I broke up with Robert. He was expecting my call. I spoke to his wife; she told me to come out. I took the plane to Munich and the bus to Salzburg; sat on the bus apprehensively. His house was divided into two: the house proper, a rather austere affair run by his wife, large rooms, marble ornaments, a grand piano at the back, nothing out of place to disturb its formal grandeur; and Ricci's studio, one floor above. The studio had its own entrance. You pressed the buzzer and up you went. Upstairs was different, Ricci's domain, one big room lined with hundreds and hundreds of CDs (mostly of him) and pictures of other violinists, photographs of his grandchildren and an advanced Bang & Olufsen stereo system flanked by massive speakers. Ricci was waiting there for me, a short man, smaller than me, dressed smart-casual, short-sleeved shirt, but looking a bit like Yoda from *Star Wars*. I played Prokofiev. It seemed to go OK. He said, "I'm giving a master class in July. Come and play for me."

I went with my sister. We were playing together a fair amount around this time. Again I played the Prokofiev solo sonata and when I had finished, he asked me to stay behind. He wanted to talk to me. "Come to dinner," he said, adding, "bring your sister." And he looked so serious I thought he was going to say, *Sorry, this won't work out.*

We went to a typical Austrian Wiener schnitzel house, wooden tables, benches, men in lederhosen. I ordered the Wiener schnitzel with potatoes, but I couldn't eat. I thought the curtain was about to come down. He said: "Listen. I want you to keep coming to me. But I don't want to take any money from you. It would be wrong. I will be learning as much from you as you will be from me. So, if you're happy with that . . ."

Happy with that! I felt embarrassed, didn't know what to say, thanked him profusely, though in the back of my mind I understood. There was a connection between us, and I could sense it, as could he. Ricci was an old man then, over eighty, but he saw a lot of himself in me. There was a real sympathy here. As he said to me later, "Only prodigies recognize prodigies." Yes, I could have paid him, but it would have made the balance between us ordinary, functional. This was going to be different. He'd lived with being a prodigy, had come through it, and had a great humor about it. He made it seem not such a big deal anymore. Of course, I wasn't a prodigy either anymore, I was twenty, but Ricci knew what I'd been through, could sense (or see) the scars. Felix, Zhislin, not one of my teachers had been a prodigy. They had been gurus. At his peak, Felix had been fantastic, able to harness the best in me, but I knew Ricci would be able to speak to me in a way no other teacher had. This is what he said about our dual lives. "First you're idolized, and everything you do is genius. But as soon as you get into your teens, then they start comparing you with yourself—they say that you're not as good as you used to be, that you're with the wrong teacher, that you don't get out and play baseball, that you look pale, you look sick, you should be in a sanatorium. From then on everything is wrong—you're not a child prodigy, you're a grown-up artist. That's why a lot of kids don't make it through those years. The only good thing about being a prodigy is that you get trained to play in front of people."

We started. The Riccis lived right in the heart of the city. Salzburg has a strange feel to it, fairy-tale architecture, quite small. It's the sort of place you long to go to when you're not there and would quite like to leave when you are. Out of season, all the concert halls and cafés are closed. The city lives in a state of splendid suspension, barely breathing. It's not the place for the lively young. Ricci didn't like it much either. He'd have much preferred teaching in London, but his post was hugely prestigious. Every two weeks, I'd fly out to Munich, take the Lufthansa bus to Salzburg and stay for four days in a youth hostel run by nuns. I would climb up the stairs and there he'd be. He had one of those big exercise balls (he had trouble with his spine) and would sit on the ball for his balance, clutching the violin in one hand, his hair all over the place. Quite a sight, and humorously defiant about his size. "I'm five foot four," he would insist, even though, standing up, he'd be looking up at me—and I am five foot two. I guess he must have shrunk. Small he may have been but I was in the presence of a living master, a player who had the largest repertoire of any violinist on stage. There was almost nothing he hadn't played—though he couldn't or wouldn't play French music. "Of course I can't play it," he'd boast. "It wasn't part of my childhood repertoire!"

What did I learn from Ricci? I didn't learn how to play the violin. I learned a lot, but it wasn't how to play. It was much more to do with trusting myself, listening to my own voice, getting the sound right. Ricci took me back to basics. I relearned all the concertos with him. He understood me completely. I could go to him about anything, and he'd know my thoughts, my doubts, almost before I'd voiced them. He knew of Zhislin. "He's not naturally gifted," he said, "and because of that, not only does he not understand it, but is very resentful of somebody who can just pick up and play." So, first of all he helped me unblock a lot of the doctrines Zhislin had drummed into me. "Just do as you want," he used to say. "Don't be dictated by fashion. You have to get rid of that voice in your head that says, 'This is what is expected, this is what the critics will like.' *Never* play to the gallery."

What I gained from Ricci was an insight into my own psyche. Felix—dear, mixed-up Felix—had seen the possibilities in me, helped my development, but Ricci simply raised me up to another level. What Ricci had, and what Felix and the others lacked, was experience of the stage, vast, decades-long experience. And that was the final link. We would talk a lot about music and the violin. He still practiced two hours a day, still had the repertoire, was completely obsessed by the violin. His wife would say to me, "Don't become like him. He's not interested in anything, except the violin!" But I liked the idea of that—for someone to have an obsession that lasts a lifetime. How many people have that? I thought it was wonderful. Ricci was encyclopedic in his knowledge: music, opera, symphonies, but he would always relate everything back to the violin, back to the thing that mattered to him the most, the vital pulse in his blood. When I was in his company I felt normal—that was it—for the first time I felt no pressure. His wife would listen to us talking together and say, "You do realize, you two, you're not normal. You think you are when you're with each other, but actually you're not." Ricci taught me that my playing was simply that: my playing. He respected what I did, how I did it, in a way that no one else ever had before. I was like him. I held the violin in my hand. I played.

Salzburg was Salzburg, full of music when the festivals were on, but not much else. I hooked up with a group of exchange students on Fulbright scholarships from Yale. We went to as many concerts as we could, every night if possible, even when we couldn't really afford them. When Jessye Norman came to town we could only stump up the cash for two tickets. Each of us got to see half the show. Real friends. Flying out, traveling in the bus with my Bergonzi, was the only part I didn't like, for there was always the question of how to appear. I had a very valuable instrument in my keep, but didn't want to show it, so I dressed down, became as inconspicuous as possible, all the while guarding it like a lioness does her cubs. I was watching but not watching, clutching it close, but trying to treat it as if it were nothing in particular.

I was aware of its vulnerability, my responsibility to it, and to myself, should anything bad happen.

But why should it? I'd started a new life, away from college, away from home too. I'd bought a flat in northwest London. Things started happening all at once. I got lucky. We had a party at my mother's house where my mother, as mothers do, insisted I play for the guests. There was a guy there, a friend of a friend. The first thing I noticed was the marvelous richness of his voice. It seemed to resonate throughout the house, floating up the stairwell. I could hear his every word. He kept on talking about who he knew, how he'd played with this conductor and that, what he could do for me. I was thinking, "Who is this guy? What does he know?" This guy turned out to be Gerald Drucker and Gerald became my fairy godfather. For thirty years he had been the principal double-bass player for the Philharmonia Orchestra. He'd started off as a violinist, but his hands were too big, and he'd moved on to the cello and then, a little later in life, the double bass. Although retired, he was very much involved in the music scene. He'd been diagnosed with cancer fifteen years before and given six months to live, but refused to let that bother him at all. He was as tall as I was small, with these huge hands and as big a smile; once I came under his wing, everything seemed to happen in a kind of glorious rush. He introduced me to his old orchestra and they sent a CD of what we played to the pianist and conductor Vladimir Ashkenazy. Ashkenazy wanted to do a concert with me. It had been a really long time since I'd done a proper, professional concert and I was scared. I was stepping back into the public arena. Without Gerald I wonder if I could have jumped back in as quickly. So it went. Ashkenazy, then the Staatskapelle Dresden . . .

Gerald gave me the confidence to be able to say in a performance, "This is how I'd like to play it." It's more difficult than you might imagine. There is the soloist and there is the accompaniment, the orchestra (though I tend to think of the solo violin as part of a larger piece of chamber music or symphony. You just happen to be the one playing it, as opposed to a section of players, that's all—and that's the pressure on you to perform). It's quite daunting to stand there in front of seventy world-class musicians who have played everything with everybody. And then there is the conductor. So, there are three of you in this relationship: the conductor, the soloist and the orchestra. Who goes first? Who determines what? You want it to be a collaboration, but it doesn't always work out like that. Conductors have egos too. If a conductor with a great reputation has a particular idea about how a concerto should be played, that's a difficulty. Sometimes it can be quite a tussle between the two people out alone on stage. I have been in several situations where the conductor has their own vision and won't deviate from it. They control the tempo, the emphasis coming from the strings and the horns and the percussion, and you have to do your best to fit in, or else the whole thing simply falls apart. Experience and rehearsals can often settle the issue, but usually we don't have much time for that. The best scenario is to have at least three live concerts back to back. By the time you get to the third, you, the conductor and the orchestra have worked things out: what this piece is, how you want to play it.

So who's in charge? Me, the soloist? The conductor? Concertos are usually only part of the whole concert. There are conductors who view the concerto as something to get out of the way, the appetizer, before the main course is served up, a nice chunk of Bruckner or whoever. That can be very frustrating. You know their mind isn't quite in tune with this. They're waiting to get the carving knife out to the meat of the matter. If you work with a conductor who used to be a violinist, either they'll be tremendously sympathetic because they know the part inside out and are with you as you explore it, or they regard it as an opportunity to play the concerto all over again in their own style. That can be a nightmare.

And the concertos don't help either. Most concertos start with the orchestra (only a few start with the violin), so, by the time you come in, the tempo has already been set. To change that tempo is hard, but there is a way, and it was Gerald who was instrumental in teaching me this technique. Obviously it depends on the layout of the piece. For example, if there is a big cadenza early on, as in the opening of Tchaikovsky, by stretching your play, pulling at the rhythm of the notes, you can change the tempo. It can be a little trickier if the orchestra has had a full run before your opportunity to influence things arises. You have to wait until the solo violin takes full stage, and that's when you can alter the pace, set it to the time that suits you. But you do it in a way that doesn't jar, just simply seems to be a natural part of the progression. And you can't do it all on your own. Gerald showed me the importance of developing a strong relationship with the leader of the orchestra. They are the fourth party in this strange triangle. An audience always sees the conductor shake the hand of the first violinist and I suspect they don't quite know why. They are just one violinist of many, maybe the best, but so what? They're not out in front but sitting behind a music stand, along with all the rest. But a good leader has tremendous influence on how an orchestra plays, how a concert can pan out. If you can establish a good rapport with them, make that connection, then they too can bring their influence to the orchestra's outlook. With the lead on your side, the orchestra following, all the poor conductor can do is to stand there, desperately trying to control this unruly beast. When that happens sparks can fly—the performance suddenly springing to an unexpected life; energy, argument, excitement filling the auditorium.

Recently I went to a London Symphony Orchestra concert. They had a new leader. He was the perfect example of the difference between a good leader and a great one. He was not only a great musician, a wonderful player, but you could sense the gift he had of being a leader—his body language open and relaxed, his energy and movement, how he somehow got inside the orchestra, lifted it up. The curious thing about music is that there is telepathy in the air. When you're playing, you're completely in tune with the subtle signals that are going around, some auditory, some visual. You absorb them all. When an orchestra is really in tune with one another, they become as one body, like I became as one body when with my violin. It's a sublime, natural rhythm and an absolute joy to be a part of. When an orchestra is in conflict with each other, you can feel it rise up from the floorboards. Turn that around and you create an energy. The best scenario of all is to have a sympathetic conductor, a sympathetic leader and an orchestra that is in tune with both your wavelengths. It doesn't happen all that often, because we're all human; good days, bad days, personality clashes, overindulgences. But when it does, then it flies.

Gerald helped transform everything, my mindset, the way I looked at things, how I felt about my playing. Hold your own, just go for it. That was Gerald's motto. *Go for it*. He got what I wanted out of myself. I had a tendency to play too fast, not because I wanted to play fast but because that's how I played: fast. It could provoke criticism, and when it did Gerald would say, "You know what? Age will take care of that." He was so right. I wish I could play that fast now! Though he never said to me, "You need to practice more"; after I met Gerald (and with Ricci waiting for me in Salzburg) I felt inspired to put in the hours to a degree that I had never done before or since. Like Ricci, Gerald was dedicated to his world, and during those years I didn't pursue any interests outside the violin. It was just about music and the violin, music and the violin. But he understood the psychology of musicians, the line of balance we have to walk, how easy it is to falter (he was credited with sweet-talking Ashkenazy back to live performance after a bout of stage fright), understood too the danger of obsession, how you could work a phrase to death. He would remind me that I wasn't a machine. "Let's take the evening off," he'd say. "Let's go to the pub."

With Ricci and Gerald, I never looked back. I was a natural again. I had my ups and downs, but they were natural, too. Something clicked into place. You get accepted, you get rejected; it's natural. When things don't align there's no point in forcing them. Gerald was instrumental in getting me my first recording, of Lalo's *Symphonie Espagnole* with ((♪₆)) the LSO. That recording led to Sony inviting me to record the Beethoven concerto. I'd started looking at it around the age of fifteen, but hadn't dared play it in public. The Brahms was the same. I'd been working with Ricci on them, marking them up, familiarizing myself with them. Playing a concerto like that is like breaking in a new pair of shoes. By the time you play it's got to fit you like calfskin.

I went on tour for War Child, playing at schools twice a week. War Child is a charity providing support to the world's most vulnerable children. I was drawn to this tour. My mother had been a war child, my father too. I'd been brought up on war-child stories. I knew what the words meant, knew the world they described. At the end of the tour we would be playing with Carl Davis and the Royal Philharmonic at Albert Hall.

But before that two things happened that I will never forget. The first, we were in Brighton, mid-January. I played the Beethoven. A few days later I received a letter from a member of the audience, a Mr. Peter Fisher. I am going to quote it here in full.

Dear Miss Min-Jin

Sixty years ago as a fourteen-year-old boy, I first heard the Beethoven Violin Concerto. I was completely mesmerized—totally enthralled. I did not realize it then, I was overawed with its sheer beauty—but now I recognize that Beethoven speaks to me in his own very special way.

At your performance on Sunday in the Dome at Brighton my thoughts and emotions were in turmoil— my love for Beethoven's concerto—a beautiful young South Korean woman who held an entire audience in thrall as she wove her own and Beethoven's magic—fifty years ago as a twenty-two-year-old infantryman fighting in the Korean war—I knew not why—and when I came home leaving my best friend buried in the United Nations Cemetery in Pusan, his young wife widowed and a baby son who never was to know his father. I thought then it was not worth it. But now fifty years after, know-

ing what South Korea has become, knowing the warmth and generosity of her people having brought into being a "display" that shows South Korea as it is now—I know that it was not in vain. And your virtuosity, so much tenderness and vitality on Sunday, brought all these thoughts flooding through my mind. Beethoven is supreme—fifty years of trauma from my soldiering in Korea—all coming together in loving consolation that brings peace.

Brava bravo, Miss Min-Jin.

Thank you, thank you, thank you, from a grateful old veteran.

It seemed to sum up why one plays: the music you bring, the emotions you feel, encourage in others, that expression of unity, of ultimate peace, that seems to be music's greatest gift. I thought of my grandparents, of what they had been through. I thought of this man who I had never met, never would meet, and yet I had reached out to him. Without knowing it I had brought him peace and happiness through recollections of chaos and confusion. That's what Beethoven allowed me to do.

Then halfway through the tour I got a call from Beare.

"We think we've found the perfect violin for you."

❧

We arranged to meet at my parents' house. It wasn't a concert hall, but at least I would get a sense of how they might play, how they might sound.

They came with a double case: two Strads. Two Strads! I'd never really imagined that I would ever own a Strad. That one case was worth more than the house we were standing in. I'd seen each violin I'd owned as a pinnacle that I'd never surpass. Two Strads!

I examined them closely. The first was a prime example of his Golden period (1700–1720). For its pedigree, it was the obvious one to go for. A handsome-looking instrument, reddish brown with hints of darker mahogany throughout. They handed it to me. I drew my bow across the strings. A deep and rich voice emerged. Could this be my voice . . . ? I played some more. Commanding, sonorous, powerful. Qualities you'd look for in the perfect instrument. I felt myself bigger, heartier, more imposing, playing this violin. But I wasn't sure. I put it down and picked up the other one.

The instant I drew the first breath with my bow I knew. It sang, so sweet and bell-like but with an underlying steel and brilliance. I was Cinderella, with her foot sticking out, the shoe gliding over the instep. It was perfect for me, so slim, so natural. That's how it felt when I lifted it, natural, the way it rested on my shoulder, how it let my fingers run across its slender neck. It was my violin. It felt as if three hundred years ago Stradivari had held his hands over a length of wood and fashioned this violin just for me, that all her life, my Strad had been waiting for me as I had been waiting for her. There was no question, no doubt. It was love at first sight, love and everything else: honor, obedience, trust, everything.

"I'm afraid you can't have it for a week," they said. "We've promised to lend it to someone in a quartet."

A week! It came to me then, that this was what my life had been leading up to—that time I'd had to wait a week for my first violin was nothing but a rehearsal for now, that it had lain within my bones, ready to respond to the resonance of the moment. All my life had been a rehearsal—the tutors, the frustrations, the loneliness, the pangs of joy: everything leading up to now, when I would meet my violin and we would begin.

How I managed I don't know, but the week went by and, at the end of it, I held it in my hands: my violin. Mine to keep.

That night I took it to my next War Child concert, along with the Bergonzi. I was to play Beethoven's Sonata No. 8 in G major. In the rehearsal I played on both. It's not normally recommended that you switch violins halfway through a tour, because experience tells you that you don't know your new violin well enough, but I tried anyway. Don't get me wrong: the Bergonzi is a beautiful instrument. I owe it a huge debt of gratitude. But this was the one. Gerald was there in the room with me. Gerald knew. Of course he knew. It was obvious to everyone. He pointed to the Strad.

"Play that one," he said.

I stepped out. I played that one. Dedicated to Tsar Alexander of Russia (the enlightened despot), Beethoven had composed Sonata No. 8 in 1802, the same year he told the world of his encroaching deafness, and his reliance on his art to overcome his despair. "I would have put an end to my life—only art it was that withheld me, ah, it seemed impossible to leave the world until I had produced all that I felt called upon to produce." Now I held the violin that would be the key to *my* art, that would will me to produce all that *I* could produce. I could hardly believe my luck. This was marriage till death do us part, made in heaven right here on earth. I was set for life.

I was twenty-one years old.

3

MASTER STRADIVARI. HIS NAME WAS ANTONIO AND HE was born in 1644 in Cremona, Italy. Cremona is a city in northern Italy, on the banks of the River Po, in what is known as Lombardy. It is a town renowned for its luthiers. Giuseppe Guarneri and several members of the Amati family also lived and worked there. The wood Stradivari used was spruce for the top, willow for the lining and the blocks inside and maple for everything else: front, back, neck. One of the strange things about the power of a top Stradivarius is exactly that: its power, its ability to fill a modern ten-thousand-seater concert hall. Was it luck or foresight that he constructed his violins so? There certainly weren't any venues of that nature back then, and yet, unlike an Amati, for instance, in a master's hand a Stradivarius can fill such an auditorium with ease. Modern instruments are purposely designed with this in mind—a stronger bass bar, a stronger bridge—but Antonio, busy in his workshop, what did he know of such things? So a Strad straddles two worlds, the ancient, the modern. There is a theory now that part of the reason for their exceptional quality is the density of the wood used—from 1645 to about 1750 the earth was experiencing a minor ice age, the trees slowing down in growth, the wood thick, heavier.

When you play a Stradivarius—a good one—you feel

the genius that was in his hands invested in the instrument. There is a touch of magic to the man who made them, the life he blew into these lumps of wood laid out on the bench, sawn and carved and planed and stuck together with glue. Pieces of wood, that's all, but when together, transformed. Pick a Strad up, play that first note, and it surges through you. You feel possessed, limitless. You are holding immortality.

This is difficult to describe on paper, the extraordinary sound a Strad can produce. In the high register it has a sweetness and naturalness—Arcadian in temperament, uncorrupted, idyllic, the harmony untainted. There is not the harshness here that you find in lesser instruments, only a blissful lightness. Nymphs bathe amid the strings. There is no restraint to its possibilities. The lower register has a richness and depth that mines the richest seams of beauty. There's burnished gold down there, waiting to be brought to light. Worlds above, worlds below, all combined in one small wooden box. And as you roam across it, from one world to the other, you find an incredible evenness of texture, a silky resonance that sweeps across the entire range, from low to high, every color in every palette lying there for you. And thus, this entrance to eternity in your hands, you are able to run the gamut of emotions, human with a voice from heaven.

I had my Strad for ten years. How do I sum them up, those years of love and happiness? A good addiction. How do I encapsulate the decade my violin and I were together? There are so many things to say, it's hard to know where to start, how to separate them all into bare paragraphs and sentences, to impose a narrative upon it, because when I think about it, it all rolls into one: the violin, me, our life together. They're not extractable moments. That would be like writing about my right leg, as if it existed as a separate entity. The violin became part of me. That's the nub of it.

Let me start with how it sits in my mind's eye: its idiosyncrasies, its imperfections, its wholeness.

It is an unusual instrument. It was made a few years before Stradivari entered his Golden period, the time when his most illustrious violins were made, the ones which are the stuff of legends—the Molitor, said to have once belonged to Napoleon, the Lady Blunt, named after Lord Byron's granddaughter and the Messiah, which resides in the Ashmolean Museum in Oxford, England. Made in 1716, the Messiah is the only Stradivarius in existence that has virtually never been played. It stayed in his workshop until his death, sold by his son Palo to a count, who then sold it in 1827 to Luigi Tarisio, himself a violin dealer and connoisseur, on Tarisio's first journey to Paris. It became Tarisio's fabled treasure. He never stopped talking about it and at one time the violinist Jean-Delphin Alard commented, "Your violin is like the Messiah: one always expects him but he never appears." The name stuck. Brahms's friend Joseph Joachim played it, struck by the melodiousness of the sound, as did Nathan Milstein in 1940, but apart from that . . . Is that a good thing or a bad thing? It's a mysterious thing, that's for sure, imbues it with a power, not unlike Wagner's *Ring of the Nibelung*, evoking both awe and desire. As the nearest example of what a Stradivarius looked like straight from the factory floor, it's unique, but as a violin it is virtually untested. Unplayed for any length of time for over three hundred years, one wonders how long it would take to awake—all the notes it had not played, all the melodies it had not heard, nothing in its memory, barely touched.

My own violin came from the period known as the Long

Pattern, so called because they were greater in length than those from the later Golden period. Mine, though it looked as long, was a little shorter than most. Whenever I had picked up a Long Pattern I had always been struck by how heavy they felt. This one was feather-light. It had a very slender body and a very slim neck. For a lot of players it would not be a comfortable instrument to hold, but it fitted me perfectly. It had been through the wars a bit. It had a hole in it, a repaired hole, but a hole nevertheless. A quarter of the front had been damaged somehow, from the top of the right-hand shoulder down, and painstakingly repaired probably two hundred years later. It bore other marks that gave it a sense of vulnerability and suffering. It had been handled badly in the past, that was clear.

I bought my Strad for a little under £450,000, part-exchanged it with the Bergonzi, raised the rest of the money remortgaging my flat. Most people use the value of the property they own to upgrade to a better one. I used it to upgrade my violin. The violin was my improved bricks and mortar, my first garden, my new balcony onto the world. Now I was determined to make it my own. Yes, it fitted me like no other, but there were adjustments I could make which would render that fit absolute. It took me months of trial and error to real-ize the right set-up. I moved the sound post a millimeter or so. It made all the difference. Now the sound filled the violin to bursting point. I shifted the bridge several times, took bits off it to make it lighter, to make it project more. The neck was quite peculiar, as I've said, extraordinarily slim, but also very deep to compensate for this narrowness. I changed the eleva-tion of the nut—the place where the string grooves are—and had the neck shaved millimeter by millimeter, so as to get its lightness, the balance in my hand, exactly right, exactly *so*. Getting it *exactly so* was everything. Perfect asymmetry.

There was a sort of enchantment waiting for us, I knew it. I experimented with a lot of different strings; I tried synthetic strings wrapped in aluminium or silver, gut strings (lamb or sheep intestines), different makes, different combinations. Synthetic strings are designed to match the rich sound of the gut, but don't require such frequent tuning. Their tone can be brighter, louder (too bright, too loud for some) but they're metal so are not subject to changes in humidity and temperature, as are gut strings. Eventually, I found a combination that seemed to work. The G string was a synthetic Thomastik string, the first synthetic string ever made, while the E string that responded best was the cheapest string available. It would last only two weeks before it started to sound tinny, but for those two weeks it produced the purest and sweetest of notes. I already had a chin rest especially made, but it took me three years to find the right bow, an 1845 Dominique Peccatte in mint condition, with the original stamp on it, perfect for the violin's weight. Even so, I had to try out different hair, different tensions before it melded perfectly. It needed to have a good spring to it, even when undone.

Bridge height, tensions, neck positions, a little slimmer here, a little heightened there, increment by increment, I molded it into my hands. If I've gone into a lot of detail here, it's because I want to stress that, wonderful as it was, it wasn't as if I opened the case and there it was, ready-made. It was there, and I could play it straightaway, but between us, we had work to do before we could realize our objective, moving toward the time when it *would* be absolute in its readiness, when I would open my case and there it would be, just like an arm or a leg, part of me. And that's what happened. It became ready. We became ready. I never had to warm up. It was there right away.

But it made me work hard. There is a paradox there, I am aware of it, my violin molded to the rest of me, yet was temperamental, some days stubborn, in a way my arm or my leg is not. That is because it is not simply a hollow block of wood. Stradivari, and all great masters like him, ancient and modern, had the capacity to breathe a life into that wood, to play a little at Frankenstein. Just look at the glow of a Stradivarius and you'll know what I mean. Just hear one when its lungs are filled. Mine was no exception, perhaps more so because of its flaws. It had a tenacious wolf note—a C which could be found on every string. A wolf note is exactly what you might imagine it to be. You play it and out comes the agonized howl of a beast. Occasionally my violin would do just that—bark. I had to learn how to play around it, deal with it. The slightest knock would open up the seams. The glue wasn't very strong. I would take it to Beare at least every two weeks because something had come undone. It didn't like the heat either. It wasn't exactly fragile, but it was sensitive. Also, it wasn't used to this way of life. Originally it had been built as a "lady's violin" (detestable phrase). Now it was starting to play big halls. I was really playing it. The soft inward voice that I'd inherited was filling bigger spaces, the violin vibrating more than it ever had before. Demands were being made on it, demands that had never been made before. I quickly learned that the best way to play it was to be as sympathetic to it as possible. Get cross, treat it with impatience, and my violin would seize up, sulk. Be kind and it would respond with a generosity that were wings to my shoulders. As Mark from

Beare once said, "It's a thoroughbred. They're sometimes temperamental!" A lot of players prefer instruments that aren't quite so demanding. Someone asked me once if, side by side, I could have a perfect version of my violin or the version that I have, which one would I choose? It's hard to say I *wouldn't* choose the perfect one, because I've never heard it, never held it, never taken it out of its case, but its imperfections were what made my violin *my* violin, what made it almost human. I needed those imperfections, needed to coax out the brilliance that lay within its damaged frame. I loved my violin, but I also had compassion for it. It had been through hard times, lived a lot. It was safe now, and my duty was to let it grow in confidence—play it as it should be played.

I was always aware of its fragility, the troubles it had been through, was determined to protect it as best I could. That's why I hated to let it out of my sight. I remember one time in Barbados. Every year, Johnny Kidd and his wife (parents of the models Jodie and Jemma) would host Holders, a world-famous performing-arts festival, on the grounds of their Barbadian plantation house, built in the seventeenth century. A stage would be set up at the end of a huge pool overlooking the polo ground, surrounded by acres of stunning gardens poised on the Caribbean Sea. In 2000, they'd booked some high-flier diva who'd canceled at the last minute. They'd had a similar kerfuffle the year before, large egos, larger demands, and had had enough of them. I got a phone call from the artistic director, asking me if I fancied a week there. My piano partner couldn't come, he was teaching, but my sister could, and as it had been a long time since we'd played properly together, it seemed an ideal opportunity to reconnect. We'd often played together when children and in our teen years, but universities (and adulthood) had separated us. We'd got back together once before, taken time exploring the classic sonatas—Brahms, Beethoven, Mozart—but not for a while. And now we could. This was why our mother wanted to come too, not as our chaperone (we were in our early twenties) but as a kind of throwback to those earlier family times. Johnny Kidd was wonderful, showed us all around the island, a marvelous host, understood too how two young women might feel, having their mother in tow. But the one thing he didn't understand was my attitude to the violin. I'd take it everywhere, wouldn't leave my room without it. It was a safe enough environment, but that cut no ice with me. So it would come to lunch with me, slung over my shoulder as I stood in line. It was there for all to see, but I didn't want to talk about it, didn't want to let on how valuable it was. Then came the rehearsals, held outside in the hot and humid air. When I picked up the violin, I could almost feel it liquefying in the heat, imagined the glue oozing out of the joints, the violin softening up, melting out of shape like a Salvador Dalí watch. I felt so guilty, subjecting it to such indignities. I refused to play outside. If I play it at all, I insisted, it had to be in the shade. Raised eyebrows. By the time of the concert, the running joke was that *I* had become the diva, the crazy girl and her bloody violin.

The concert took place in the evening, nice and cool. We both behaved ourselves.

I'd never felt like that with another human being, never said, "That's it, you're the one." But with the violin that's *exactly* how I felt. You *are* the one. There's a kick when I write that, a kick that makes it hard for me to revisit my time with the violin. I'd met my soulmate. That is why writing about those ten years is so hard. Every time I try to get close to them, there's a buzzing in my head. Something presses down on me, or is it trying to get out? Like the dream I have, it's hard to say. Wherever it comes from, it's the barrier between who I am and who I was and it returns every time I try to go back to it—it was a change of life and my body doesn't like it. I go into shock, shut down, forget how to fashion words. When I write about it, it's as if I am writing about a different person, a person who no longer exists. I talked differently then, I thought differently. I saw the world in different colors, different sounds. It was a different world. The violin brought me experiences and thoughts and feelings that only my violin could bring. When you are close to someone, spend all your time with someone, you pick up on their idiosyncrasies, their habits, their outlook, their voice. That was me and my violin.

If this chapter could be music I'd build up to a crescendo of security and happiness, remembering the good times, remembering its glorious silky voice and the fit on my shoulder, like an embrace. That's what it brought me, security and happiness, the closest thing to me. I never questioned the singularity of that. That's what it was. It made me weightless, limitless. I never questioned my existence. The violin *was* my existence. There was not one single moment when I didn't want to play. I was back in the world that I had experienced as a young child, only now I was grown up and in charge, with the object of my love and experience and future safe in the case beside me. I would take it out, tune it up and I would be me.

I made my first recording with the independent company Claudio Bohemia. Bohemia is a passionate label that does only what it believes in. I played Lalo's *Symphonie espagnole.*

Ricci chose the Lalo and for me it was full circle, my debut recording reprising my first public performance. The Lalo was my calling card. Gerald sent it off to Sony. I'd stepped up on the merry-go-round, ready for the ride. Could I handle it, keep my balance?

The first test came right after that first recording. The very next day I had a concert with the Royal Liverpool Philharmonic, playing Tchaikovsky. The recording had taken three days, and after a thing like that, normally you'd take a rest. It's an exhausting process. You're in the studio all day, two long, intense recording sessions. It sounds like a physical thing (and you need to be in some sort of shape) but, as Ricci had warned me, "It's not the physical strength, Min, it's the mental stamina that counts—you need to pace yourself." Yet nothing had quite prepared me for the reality of that demand, the hour-after-hour intensity of concentration, the focus absolute. We finished at around seven o'clock, and I'd begun to panic. The concert was less than twenty-four hours away. I told Gerald I had to go home. "I've got a concert tomorrow. I have to practice." Gerald took one look at me and said, "Bad idea. Go to sleep. You'll be fine."

Next morning I drove down for the concert, a long drive. Before I knew it, I was out on stage, violin in hand, Tchaikovsky waiting in the wings. I was still tired. But things kick in. Your fingers know what they're doing. They're not on automatic pilot exactly, but they're carrying a lot of the work for you. You don't have to worry about them. If you do, it's all over. (There's a revealing clip on YouTube of Maria João Pires settling down at the piano, ready to perform one of Mozart's piano concertos for a lunchtime concert in Amsterdam. Only she's prepared for the wrong one, and as the music starts up, she turns, a look of despair on her face. The conductor, Riccardo Chailly, grins, waves her worries away with the words, "You know it so well," and carries on. And Maria João Pires, utter professional that she is, gathers herself together, waits for the moment, turns back to the piano and makes her entrance perfectly. Her fingers know what to do. She plays the piece without a hitch.) How the concert went I really can't remember. But Gerald had been absolutely right. If I'd practiced that night before, the concert would have been a disaster. But I'd given myself and the violin a little breathing space; let what I knew, what it knew, lead me there.

At the end of the concert my mother said, "You know, it struck me tonight, you really *can* play the violin!" That may sound like a strange thing for a mother to say, but for her, who so rarely put her emotions into words, it was extraordinary and powerful. It made me feel loved. I thought: That wasn't just me on stage. It was all the other things that I'd worked with and worked toward, Ricci and Felix and Gerald, work and practice and knowledge that had seeped into me and my violin. I knew every curve of that violin, and it knew me. There was memory in that wood as well as in my fingers. Heifetz once finished a concerto, held his violin and kissed it. We all know that feeling. It's the difference between a good violin and a great one. A good one, you have to work hard to make it sound right. If you're tired or not as well prepared as you'd like to be, you're going to be below par. But a great violin can never let you down in that way. It knows. It's a thoroughbred. It inspires you, carries you both across the line.

You might think all this Stradivarius stuff is an exaggeration. Surely they can't be that good. The fact is, they are. It's personal, which is why violinists rarely like anyone else playing their instrument. The only person I allowed to play my violin in those ten years was Ricci himself. He had been invited to give a concert at the Musical Instruments Museum in Cremona. They had an extraordinary collection of Strads—and they'd asked Ricci to play them all. It was a fairly high-powered gathering—all the famous luthiers, dealers, those in the know. Right at the end, he said, "My student has a Strad," and he asked me if he could play it. I said I'd be honored (and so would my violin). He played the Bach Partita No. 2, and guess what? The audience liked my Strad above all the others. The baby! The concert over, it was bees around a honeypot, all of them looking at it, wanting to touch it, get a piece of the action. Quite a number offered me money for it there and then. I was horrified, clutched it close. "It's not for sale. Absolutely not!"

With Ricci and Gerald as my guides I focused hard now on relearning the violin repertoire. I'd got my wings. I was the pilot. I could fly the plane. I could take the controls, and I could fly it. It was smaller than a plane, but it could take me there, physically and mentally. I went all over. South Africa, Korea, America. I've heard it said that when flying in the heavens, the pilot feels a great sense of ease and well-being, that for all the demands made upon him or her, the knowledge of where they are, the sight of it, brings a sense of safety, security. It's the world they know, the world only they truly inhabit. I lived in a similar singular world with my violin. It was my passport. My livelihood, the means by which I traveled and marked the world, but it was also my place of safety. In Los Angeles, hugely exciting for me, but also a weirdly discombobulating culture shock, I would need to shut myself in a small room and practice with my violin in order to feel normal again, to feel safe. I needed my violin. Like my old box room back at my parents' house, I needed a haven I could retreat to, the place where my sense of self and self-reliance could be established again.

And things took off. It seems a blur now, unreal, as if it hardly happened to me, for those times belong to a world that this Min no longer inhabits. It was hard going, but that didn't seem to matter much. You've no time to think. You learn the repertoire at the same time you're playing concerts. No time to dwell on anything else. And I didn't. It was tough, but there was a smoothness to it, a path that was clearing.

The only bad thing that happened took place closer to home. I was staying at someone's house, a woman I'm very close to. I had my violin with me, of course. I had a friend with me, who wanted me to go and see their new flat. I asked if I could leave my violin in the house while I did. It would be much safer there, indoors, than carrying it around London. The woman said no, take it with you. It was strange, unlike her, but she was insistent. So I took it, a little put out.

There'd been a party going on in the flat below hers. Someone saw me leave, thought I was the owner. My friend went to bed early, and woke to hear noises in the bathroom. Imagining I had returned, she got up, and came face-to-face with a man. Terrified, she pleaded with him to take whatever he wanted, but he'd already done that. He was just checking to see if he'd missed anything. He left, and with him went the woman's passport, her briefcase, her music case, everything he could lay his hands on. He could have taken my violin, *would* have taken my violin. What had possessed her to insist I take it? What had possessed me to agree? My relief was tempered by the strangeness of it all—almost as if life were telling me how chance and fate and opportunity are intangibles. Never let me go. That was something I could write on the case.

Ricci was getting old. His health had started to suffer. The winters in Salzburg are cold and damp and long. His wife decided it would be best for them to move to Palm Springs. It's a place where a lot of elderly people in poor health retire to. He was eighty-five, no longer earning. So they sold the violin he'd had for fifty years, and moved. I would fly over every three months or so, spend a week in his house. I could have been his daughter. One day he started talking to me about how much he missed his violin. He was playing on a modern instrument by then. "Shall I tell you a secret, Min?" he said. "I've had three wives but only one violin." I knew how he felt. Ginette Neveu would have known how he felt. Your violin was for life. It *was* your life. You'd happily die with it in your arms.

Ricci invited me along to a master class he was giving in LA for the Heifetz Society, a non-profit organization, conceived and co-founded by Claire Hodgkins and Sherry Kloss (both longtime teaching associates of Heifetz). He wanted me to play a piece at the end of the class, naturally I agreed, I played Chausson's *Poème*. Claire came up to me afterward and said she wanted to hear more. Did I have any recordings? I gave her the Lalo. A few weeks later, when I was back in the UK, she rang me to say that the society wanted to award me the Heifetz Prize. It wasn't a cash prize. Instead it was a lifetime's worth of career promotion beginning with a recital at the Alex Theatre in LA.

A year later I arrived, ready to give my debut. About two hours before the concert I realized I had forgotten to pack my concert shoes. The only other footwear I had was a pair

((♪7))

of trainers, not suitable. We had to drive to the mall and buy something decent. Coming back we got caught in the traffic, and made it back to the theater with only moments to spare. Claire saw how breathless I was, how out of tune with what I was about to do. She sat me down in my dressing room, and told me that I wasn't going out until I had my breath back. I protested, but, like Gerald before her, she was right. Poised, controlled, unflappable, for a while she became like a second mother to me, always ringing me up from her home in LA to see how I was getting on, planning my future and my career. I learned a lot from Claire, about Heifetz, his work ethic, his philosophy, even his diet. He was the most influential violinist of his time, every player after him has a little bit of Heifetz in them, whether they know it or not.

Winning the Heifetz was the highlight of my young career, a huge but scary honor. The society had spent six years searching for a recipient who they felt represented Heifetz's ideals, so for them to single me out was overwhelming. For many people Heifetz typifies everything a violinist should be. There was a well-known ailment that affected violinists of his generation known as Heifetzitis, the impossibility of playing anything other than Heifetz. Ricci used to say that Heifetz played bad music amazingly well and great music quite badly. We used to laugh at it because we both knew what he meant. Heifetz was Heifetz. He played only Heifetz, couldn't help it. Playing has changed over the forty years since he was such a dominant force, but back then the personality of the player was as important as the interpretation of the music. For Heifetz that was both a blessing and a curse because he knew his reputation, was fed up with being accused of being cold, playing with that poker face. As an experiment, he once took a number of recordings by different violinists, himself included, and played them to an unsuspecting group of musicians and nonmusicians, to see which player got the greatest emotional response. Without exception, Heifetz was chosen every single time. Of course! He's so high octane, so intense. Listen to him play the Mozart Sonata in B-flat major. It's not Mozart at all, completely wrong, but at the same time, absolutely wonderful, absolutely right. Nobody else could get away with it, but—it's Heifetz! Even Kreisler was stunned by his performances, saying when he first heard the twelve-year-old play the Mendelssohn concerto, "We may as well break our fiddles across our knees."

I knew I couldn't have done it without my violin. It was because of my violin that I could reach those heights. We were in full flow, and I was happy. (A digression: as well as an unassailable career as one of the greatest violinists that has ever lived, Heifetz moonlighted as the "Tin-pan Alley" songwriter Jim Hoyle, most notably writing "When You Make Love to Me (Don't Make Believe)," sung by Bing Crosby with the Victor Young Orchestra. I love this story. It brings out the light-hearted quality of his character—quite different from the austere, po-faced master he is so often portrayed as.)

Sony had liked what they heard. They came back to me. Would I like to record the Beethoven? Sony UK would release it first, and then, with an additional track of Ricci's arrangement of Tárrega's *Recuerdos de la Alhambra*, Sony Korea would follow with their own promotion and a huge tour. Nine months later, Sony's release day came and I was thrown into the deep end, seven-to-seven, back-to-back interviews every fifteen minutes, then a concert, a big one at Seoul's Art Center, about two thousand people. Like my time in LA, I needed the violin just to keep me sane, the place I could retreat to. How healthy that dependence was I cannot say, but a soloist's life is by its very nature one where being alone is paramount. That's what you are. A singer is a singer, a painter is a painter, a writer is a writer. But a soloist is exactly that, always standing alone, always apart. That's the job description. There is no other reason for their existence. And in the case of the soloist and the violin? Through its shape, its sound, its weight, its look, its availability, it's the intimacy you crave, you need—and you have. Enough.

We've reached the year now, 2010. I was thirty-one. Life was good. My playing was gathering maturity, my performance schedule gathering momentum. I rode with it. I had family, I had friends, I had people I could rely on, depend on. And then one of those rocks was taken away. Gerald died.

I still feel it. For those ten years Gerald had been perhaps the most important figure and voice in my life. A truly special human being—with his strength of character, his wisdom, his courage, he was, and remains, a guiding force in every decision I make. There was a sort of goodness within him that shone forth like a beam of light guiding you away from danger or self-delusion. I remember very early on in our friendship, sitting in his living room, just talking about life—and as we chatted away, I felt the room glow with a golden warmth that was Gerald's spirit. We spoke daily on the telephone, and I would play for him once a week, whatever I was working on. While he was encouraging and would gently ask me, in his soft but rich and warm voice, the right questions to develop my interpretative musical mind, he never really interfered with my musical intention. He believed, as Ricci did, that the most important thing was to listen to instinct and play as you feel. His experience, working with some of the greatest musicians over several generations, was staggering, but he was unassuming and humorous. I don't have a godfather but Gerald filled this gap, became my musical and spiritual guide. He was the first person I would call about anything new happening, good and bad and everything in between. If this sounds like a eulogy, so be it. He deserves one.

The blur gathers speed. After the Beethoven came Sony's offer that I record the Brahms. I hadn't been completely happy with the Beethoven recording—so this time I insisted on listening back to everything. Recording music like Brahms is a marriage between the old world and the modern way of playing—the set-up. For instance, how much reverb you use depends on the engineer, the producer, even the record label. In the eighties, when it was the new thing, they went mad for it. I don't like too much reverb. For me the natural reverb of the room is enough.

I practiced hard for the Brahms. Years back you could count on having any number of rehearsals before the recording, but current commitments, expenses, don't allow for that. A player gets one or two, three at the most. So I put a lot of preparation in. I knew the work, had studied countless different interpretations. Now it was my turn. I locked myself away to prepare for it with only my cats Billy and Lilly and my recording equipment for company. (Have I mentioned my cats before, my wonderful Burmese cats, Billy and Lilly? Billy's lilac and Lilly's blue. They love each other as I do them. The Dynamic Duo.) In the weeks leading up to the recording, I didn't go out at all, stayed in, playing, practicing, eating on the hoof. Then a friend of mine gave me a wonderful break, inviting me down to his rented villa in the South of France. It was the perfect place to relax and still come to grips with the great flow of Brahms' music, perhaps the best place. There'd be his family in their infinity pool, swimming the afternoon away, and I'd be upstairs with the windows open, playing the Brahms, playing the Brahms, playing the Brahms. By the time the recording came, I was ready.

My producer was Andrew Keener. Andrew is one of the most experienced producers, and the recordings he has overseen are a testament to his genius for tuning in to artists, harnessing their strengths and ambitions, understanding how they work. I like to take three complete runs at a work before editing. This makes the recording as near to a live performance as possible. My intention was to be as spontaneous with the Brahms as I could. I trusted Andrew's perspective. "Just try this," he would say, and though I might demur at first I often found that he was absolutely right. The first movement has a series of stunning arpeggios that flow from one idea to another. Like the Beethoven, I see this work as a huge piece of chamber music. The orchestra has the line, the shape, and the soloist brings the ornamentation to that line, weaving in and out of it. It was an emotional perspective that we were going for. Likewise the last movement has a very rhythmic foundation, and while I needed to keep that, I wanted it to be more of a dance, an expression of joy.

But it is the second movement, the movement we recorded first, which lies both geographically and emotionally at the heart of this work. Brahms wrote his violin concerto in 1878, and it was first performed, as planned, a year later, on New Year's Day (a month before Kreisler's fourth birthday!). His longtime friend and collaborator, the violinist and composer Joseph Joachim, had played a large part in its composition (Brahms could be cavalier about fingering and bowing). The premiere took place in Leipzig, a rather deadline-hurried affair, and it wasn't until after furious revisions by both composer and player that the concerto found its rapturous reception two weeks later in Vienna.

Brahms wrote this movement as a love letter to his great unrequited love, Clara Schumann. Clara herself was a prodigiously talented pianist. She made her debut at nine, performed her first solo concert at eleven (how the lives of prodigies echo through the centuries), and took Vienna by storm when she was just eighteen years old. Her love affair with Robert Schumann, a fellow student, was bitterly opposed by her father—he took them to court to try to stop their marriage—but married they were, just before her twenty-first birthday. Though their love was deep and enduring, Schumann was a deeply troubled soul, and however hard Clara tried, she couldn't keep the demons that haunted and taunted him at bay. Brahms first met the couple in 1853, he an aspiring young composer come to pay court to the great man. Their rapport was almost immediate. Schumann, along with Clara, became great champions of Brahms's talent. Schumann saw in him a possible successor to his own legacy, and perhaps more besides—for the great tragedy was that Schumann was fully aware of the madness lying semi-dormant within him, and knew that it would eventually devour him. A year after Brahms and Schumann first met, it struck. Schumann tried to drown himself in the Rhine. Pulled out, he was committed to an asylum in Enderich, near Bonn, which he would never leave. When Brahms started to fall in love with Clara is unclear, but by the time of Schumann's suicide attempt, and although there was fourteen years' difference between them (she was thirty-six, he twenty-two), it was clear that theirs was an intense and deeply felt friendship. Months later, after Clara had given birth to her son Felix (named after Mendelssohn), Brahms wrote to a friend, "I can no longer love an unmarried girl . . . they only promise heaven while Clara shows it revealed to us." It was a love he, and also she, were determined to suppress.

In the two years that followed, Brahms became Clara's near-constant support. He stayed at the Schumanns' house. They played and talked music together. He looked after her children while she busied herself earning money with constant recital tours. They went on chaperoned holidays together. Although she was forbidden by the doctors to attend, he was a regular visitor to the asylum, all the while a young man struggling to find his own voice as a composer; two voices within him—the artist, the lover—desperate to get out. Only once did he ever write to Clara of his feelings, even then masking them by reciting a tale from *A Thousand and One Nights*, ending with the words, "I am dying for love for you. Tears prevent me from saying more."

On his twenty-third birthday in 1856 he visited Robert Schumann and found him deteriorating fast. The end was near. The doctors allowed Clara to visit her husband for the first time. With Brahms standing by her side, she knelt by his bed, stroked his brow, fed him jellied consommé with her fingers. A day later, as they both traveled back from Bonn, having collected their mutual friend Joseph Joachim, they returned to find Schumann dead. At the funeral two days later, Brahms carried Clara's wreath to the grave.

It was expected by many, by Clara too, that they would marry, but now Brahms made the choice that defined his career and their love. He could choose life with Clara or he could choose music. He chose music. He left. Years would pass. Their relationship would fluctuate as the seasons, tranquil one moment, turbulent the next, but she was always Clara, always there wherever he went, whatever he did, the love that had been denied him, the love he had denied himself. In 1856 he wrote to her that he felt unable to connect his music to his heart, but by the time he wrote his violin concerto, those wires were all in place, Brahms the elder master of form fused to Brahms the young Romantic. The pent-up years of longing and misunderstandings all came to fruition in this most woundingly perfect of all concerto movements—an astonishing outpouring of love and loneliness. To hear this music, to know this music, to play this music is to define, in music, the state of love. To play this, for me and my violin, was just that. Love. Others play it differently, others see it differently, but this is how I feel. Never able to fulfill his inner longing for her, there it all lies on the page, Johannes Brahms's Violin Concerto in D major, Op. 77—the notes, the diagrams, the instructions. This is what my violin was made for. This is what I was made for. This is what we are made for—this single movement.

Right at the end of the slow second movement, there are two repeated up-bow Cs, so it accords with the orchestra, we're in unison, the second C dying away. And as I played the resolving note that follows, the note wouldn't come out, my violin suddenly stubborn, digging its heels in. So I gave it a little nudge and . . . BARK, out it came. We could have rerecorded the section, but I wanted to keep it in. It was bringing the recording close to a live performance and, besides, it was my violin's concerto too.

I was happy with the people I worked with, particularly the oboist Gordon Hunt (the Brahms concerto is sometimes jokingly referred to as the "Oboe Concerto" on account of that instrument's prominence). Gordon's phrasing, the balance he drew between sentiment and rigor of intention, encapsulated that bittersweet longing that Brahms was expressing.

I recorded the Brahms in the summer. It would take six months to edit. Sony planned to release it in December and, as with the Beethoven, built the release around a concert tour. In the meantime I had embarked on a series of concerts with the London-based Philharmonia Orchestra, going around the country, performing in regional concert halls. I was also in a relationship now. We hadn't been seeing each other long— three months. I'd met him at the Open Chamber Music Seminar held in Prussia Cove near Porthleven in Cornwall, which takes place every September for three weeks. Friends and colleagues from all over the world come together to take part in master classes and concerts.

Prussia Cove is one of the most magical places on earth, and the festival that Steven Isserlis, the artistic director, holds there is a mecca for serious-minded musicians who want to work and have fun at the same time. You're there for a week and it's an intense seven days. Musicians are divided up into chamber groups of three, four or five, and you work together. At the end of the week you're given the option of playing before an audience. There's no pressure, it's up to you and your group to decide whether you're ready or not, but nevertheless it's very full-on, a week of almost constant playing— nine o'clock to one, then an hour for lunch and then either rehearsing until the evening, or taking the afternoon off before rehearsing in the evening. However you call it, it's music all day, and when you're not rehearsing you're talking music or playing impromptu. The atmosphere is intoxicating. You get caught up, find yourself still playing at two in the morning, captured in Prussia Cove's spellbinding web.

I'd been invited before, but you have to be able to commit to the whole week, Sunday to Sunday, and this year was the first time my diary was completely free. Initially I was meant to go with a pianist friend but something came up and he couldn't make it. I nearly pulled out, for I wouldn't know anyone there, I would have to do that thing that didn't come easily to me—socialize, be outward, on show. But then I thought, It would be crazy not to. I'd be bound to make friends.

The festival is made up in the main of professional musicians, but there are also a handful of students who get picked by their professors. This is the route that Matt had taken. And Matt was the cellist in our little chamber group. He was younger than me, excited to be there—his bounce and enthusiasm delightful and infectious. He was soft-spoken, funny and friendly, good-looking too, with his thick black hair and his Maltese-family complexion. We were rehearsing Janáček's *Intimate Letters*—all about the composer's obsession with a younger woman, and that week Matt took the music to heart, inverted the age discrepancy and wouldn't leave me alone. When I sat down for breakfast there was Matt. When we had lunch there would be Matt, about to sit next to me. Everywhere I looked, Matt, Matt, Matt.

One time early on, Matt asked me if I wanted to go for a walk after lunch, said he knew a really pretty path that led to a secret beach. It sounded like a lovely idea and we headed off. The path was very beautiful, rugged rocks leading down to a sandy beach, the sea to our right, wild flowers and straw-like grass all around. I hadn't explored this side of the estate yet and we walked in silence; it was sunny but windy and my hair had got loose and was whipping around my face. Suddenly Matt stopped walking and looked at me and said: "You should wear your hair down more often. It looks nice like that." I was a bit embarrassed. It was a bit more personal than I had imagined.

"Thanks," I said.

He went on, "I've got a confession to make."

A confession! This wasn't what I had expected at all.

"OK. What is it?"

"I actually thought about emailing you before Prussia Cove when I found out we were playing together, but kept chickening out. So in case you noticed loads of hits on your website from the same IP address, I'm afraid that was me cyber-stalking you!"

I kept it light.

"I didn't notice," I said, "but you should have definitely written to say hi!"

"Yes, I can see that now . . ." he said. Out it came. I was too distant, but the moment he saw me, he could see that I was totally approachable. He recognized my vulnerability. It was the thing he liked best in me. My weak side, my human side.

Whoa! Over the top, slightly scary? If anyone had said that to me in real life after three days of meeting up I think I would have kept them at a distance, but Prussia Cove was a bubble—a magical bubble, and no more fixed to the gravity of everyday life than the moon. It was easy to lose one's perspective. Again, I didn't quite know what to say, mumbled some sort of thanks.

He said, "I've told you my secret. Now you have to tell me something too . . . Anything. Otherwise we're not even!"

He was making connections, him and me, some ground to share, I could see that, didn't run away from it.

"Well, this morning I was half asleep and I thought I felt a presence in the room . . ."

Was that wise? Too late now.

"You mean like a ghost?" he said, half laughing. "Were you scared?"

"Actually, no. It was quite a friendly spirit, a warm matronly atmosphere—like she was welcoming me into her home . . ."

He asked me which cottage I was staying in. I told him. Cliff Cottage. He became serious.

"Didn't you know? The whole estate is haunted."

I thought he was teasing me. He assured me he wasn't.

"Loads of people have seen ghosts here," he said. "Hilary [the founder of OCM at Prussia Cove] can tell you all about it."

Whether it was populated with ghosts or not, I didn't want him going around telling everyone what I'd admitted to.

"I haven't met half the people here yet," I said, "and I don't want this to precede me!"

He held up his hand. "I promise."

We finished our walk. Later that evening a fellow cellist teased me about the story. I was a little put out and jokingly said to Matt that I would never trust him again. But I didn't take it seriously.

The days progressed. I found his determination attractive,

compelling. It was a good feeling, not being on my own. I could laugh at it too, this male single-mindedness, and laughter does a lot of things, breaks down a lot of barriers. A lot of people found it funny too, how he wouldn't let anyone else get near me. Not everyone, though. There was a girl there who warned me off him, said Matt had a bit of a reputation with Korean girls. It all sounded rather over the top to me, rather unfair, telling tales out of class. They weren't going to spoil it for me.

We became friends. Matt was a good player but I could see that the life of a full-time musician was not going to be for him. He knew it too, and was realistic about it. But he was ambitious. His goal was to become part of the dealing fraternity. It was a sensible idea. If he worked as a dealer, it would give him the best of both worlds: a solid income, while keeping him firmly attached to the musician's world he loved. He'd already made some important connections. While a student studying in Rochester, New York, he'd hooked up with a young dealership, Tarisio, a firm named after Luigi Tarisio of the famous Messiah. The firm was just starting out, and there was room for an enthusiast like Matt. So every weekend he'd take the train to New York and help out the luthiers, no pay, just a willing foot in the door. But that was Matt all over: determined, relentless, focused on getting what he wanted. To that end, he'd brought the director of Tarisio, Jason Price, to come down to Prussia Cove to show all the players the instruments he was going to auction that season. He was good with people that way, good at making connections, getting the most out of them, putting himself in the frame.

The week came, the week went. At the end there's a long-standing tradition the musicians have, going back to

London on the train. They take over a carriage and as they leave Penzance order up a mess of pizzas to be delivered to a station farther down the line. It's been done for years, so when they get the call, the pizza firm knows exactly what to do. It sounds standoffish of me, but after the hectic rush of the week, all I wanted was to rest up, sleep a little, and so I had booked a seat in the quiet carriage to do just that. And I'd just settled down, when up popped Matt again. He'd left the party, wanted to join me. I told him, "No, go and enjoy yourself," but he was Matt, persistent. He sat down. We talked about this and that, drifted off to sleep. Every now and again one of the girls from the party would burst in, try to drag him back to the fun, but he'd say, "No, Min wants me to stay here." It's not what I'd said at all, I was happy for him to go, but in time I learned that it was a very Matt thing to say, to put the onus on someone else, never himself.

Back on terra firma, his persistence won me over. My defenses came down. We got together. He lived in Manchester; I still had my flat in Harrow. When we could, we'd divide our time between the two, a week down south, a week up north. Up and down we'd go, Matt always by my side. I finished the concert series, was giving myself time to prepare for the release of my CD, due out around Christmas. Sony had plans for concerts all over Korea. Matt was studying for his masters at the Royal Northern College and I'd wound down my performances. It was easy for me to travel back and forth.

We're getting close now. Only a couple of months to go. I was with Matt up in Manchester a good deal. We'd only been together for a few weeks, but I was already becoming a little unsure of him. He was six years younger than me, a mature student. I was about to embark on a promotional tour for my forthcoming CD. We were in very different places in life. Sometime soon I might want to start thinking about settling down, but he was nowhere near any of that. And I started seeing things in Matt that weren't really for me. He was good with people, yes, but perhaps a little too good, getting them to do what he wanted. Everything was done with Matt in mind. He seemed possessive to a degree, something my friends found disturbing. Maybe I was growing out of that need for dependence: maybe when I looked at our relationship, without fully realizing it I was seeing a reflection of what people had done to me year after year and didn't like what I saw. I had a sense of something, that's for sure. Maybe, for a brief moment, I was ready to stand on my own two feet, Min and her violin and whatever the world outside had to offer. I was a performer on the world stage, I had a place of my own, friends of my own. Like Ricci, I'd just about got through it all. I'd only known Matt for a couple of months. It should be easy enough to cut loose, not too many scars on either side. I didn't dislike him, but I knew this relationship wasn't for me. I expressed my doubts, laid the groundwork. He'd say, "My parents got married when they were twenty," and I liked that. It was an endearing observation—that rawness, uncertainty could be the basis of something strong, lasting. After all, that's what my parents did too. We stayed together. Late October.

The week before, I'd given my last concert, playing the Schubert Piano Trio in B-flat major. The violin suited Schubert, the poignant taste that runs through that music, particularly in the slow movement. It was a pleasing thing to finish on. This week, though, I wasn't well. I'd caught a chest infection, had fainted in the street on the way to buy antibiotics and was now pumped up with steroids the paramedics had given me. Matt had to go to Lewes, on the Sussex coast. He was on a Feldenkrais course down there. Feldenkrais is a somatic educational system which aims to reduce pain or limitations in movement. A lot of musicians use it. It works to promote a general sense of well-being by increasing a student's awareness of themselves, and expanding their movement repertoire. In some countries it's part of their physical educational system. Perhaps the nearest thing we have in common use here is the Alexander Technique. Matt was hoping to become a Feldenkrais teacher. I didn't feel like traveling (a friend had invited me for dinner, and in truth I'd have rather gone to that), but Matt was insistent. It was important to him that I went with him. So I did. I went to Lewes, spent the weekend there, still not 100 percent.

That Monday we traveled back to London, stopped off at my flat. It was cold in the flat and we were hungry. We were due to catch the train back to Manchester at around nine o'clock that evening from Euston. Matt had the idea of going to the station early for a bite to eat. It's not something I would do normally, but medication and tiredness and the chill of unheated rooms are not the best counsels for decision making. I did what he wanted. I didn't want to, but I did it. It was getting to be a habit with me.

Something bad is about to happen. There is no point in going through the what-ifs, the possibilities that could have changed everything: what does it do but increase your sense of guilt, stupidity? But when something bad happens you do it all the same. I do it all the time, still to this day, the fire I could have lit, the other café we could have chosen, the argument we need not have had. I should have been stronger. I should have been me. But I wasn't that me. I was the me who was going to do these things, make those choices or have those choices made for me. Here we go. It's six-thirty on a dark, first-of-November night, 2010. There's cold and wind and damp in the air. We're destined for Euston, leaving an hour or so before we have to. We're in Harrow now, but I'm just closing the door, getting into the taxi. I'm carrying a suitcase and my violin case. Matt is carrying a suitcase and a cello case. We duck our heads and settle in; a short ride to the tube, a short ride to Euston.

See you there.

❧

Up we come, out of the Underground and into the jaws of the station. I'm not feeling too well, still on those heavy-duty steroids. The weekend has left me exhausted—the ride over too. I shouldn't have gone to Lewes, shouldn't be doing this, any of it. I know it in my bones, but Matt is insistent. Opposite, the entrances to the platforms yawn at me, demanding descent. It's all too much: the crowds, the announcements, the clamorous rush. All I want to do is sit down. We turn, walk now to the mall outside, the open-air tables forlorn and empty, puddles on the seats. There's a parade of restaurants lined up: Ed's Diner, Nando's, Caffè Nero, Café Rouge; hot dogs, burritos . . . None of them seems very appetizing, but we might as well choose one, now we're here. We go into Ed's Diner, stand in the doorway by the cardboard-cut-out woman with her smile and her red skirt and her all-American tray, but it's cramped and noisy, and besides there's no real room for our luggage, luggage consisting of two suitcases, one cello worth around a quarter of a million pounds and a violin worth nearly four times that amount. It's in my hand now, safe in its sturdy case, my life and my life's two bows, and my life's spare strings.

We go back outside, into the cold again. Across the walk divide is a Pret A Manger. There's a table free, by the entrance. (This is important. There are two entrances: this one, leading directly to the railway station; and another, leading to the bus station, around the back of the restaurant and quite out of sight.) It's busy, but where isn't? They're not made for rest, these places. Matt secures the table, putting all the luggage and his cello between the window and the table. I go to the counter. I buy a hot meatball sandwich and a cup of tea for myself, and a soup for Matt. When I get back Matt has rearranged his luggage so that his cello is behind the suitcases, nearer him. I sit opposite, with my violin case between my legs, the strap around my ankle. It's how I always sit, *always*, the violin by my side, in sight/out of sight, but *with the strap around my ankle*. It's part of me, remember, as personal and as intimate as any other. (I remember, one time, the shock of violation I felt when, waiting to give a concert, the conductor came into my dressing room and, without a word, lifted my violin out of its case and started plucking at the strings—that he should touch me so, that he felt he had the right . . .) But it's safe now.

So here I am sitting, feeling lousy, the strap around my ankle.

Matt says, "You look really uncomfortable."

I sigh. The truth is I probably *am* uncomfortable, tired,

not feeling great; the journey, the weekend, all of it a bit pointless. I snap.

"What now?"

Matt says, "I think the violin should be here."

I suggest we swap places. I want the violin with me, but Matt doesn't warm to this idea. He doesn't want to swap places. He thinks he should be sitting with the luggage and his cello. What he wants is for me to put my violin alongside his cello and the rest of the luggage. I say, "No way!" He is insistent. We argue, back and forth, participate in that dread event, the private row broadcast to everyone within earshot, an act of both fascination and embarrassment for the unwilling audience. It's something you don't do in public, in railway stations, in restaurants, in a Pret A Manger café on a cold November night. Back and forth the argument goes, where he wants it, where it should go, if only I could see myself (how true *that* is), more and more pressure. Finally, I relent, following the pattern of acceptance that is our default position—the pattern of acceptance I have always fallen into, Min giving way, Min obeying, Min dependent for support on the object strapped to her foot, or tucked underneath her chin, or residing, half dormant, in its Ricci-donated case.

So, insistence wins. Again. I hand over the violin. Matt places it in a gap between one of the suitcases and the glass window, but I am unhappy with that. More argument, more embarrassment. Eventually, he agrees to move it, to put it next to him. Words fly into my mouth, words so weak, so without resolve, that it pains me to remember them. I ask him to promise me that he'll look after it. After I've given it away, I ask him to look after it! Too late. It's out of my hands now.

At this moment, I do not see the sharks circling outside. I do not know of the three men who have walked up and down the concourse as we have, looking into the restaurants as we have, do not see the way they scan the area, how they move on to where there may be better pickings. I do not see them, though they are probably here already, standing inside or looking through the window, conferring by nods and shrugs and the meetings of eyes. If I did, I might have noticed that they have trained their focus on a woman's handbag a few tables from us. She chats on to her friend, quite unaware, as am I, of their intent. It won't matter to her though, this un-awareness we share. In a few moments she will walk away, unscathed, intact, while I . . . So, unaware, she saves her handbag, does something equally unaware, shifts her body perhaps, or puts a finger on the bag's clasp. Maybe it comes from the person with her, or the couple opposite. Whatever it is, whoever it comes from, the confluence of opportunity changes. The men's eyes drift away, scan the room, fall on me. Or rather they fall on the part of me that is no longer with me. They fall on my violin.

(Do they know it's a violin? It can't be worth much, surely, judging by the two who accompany it. Maybe they think it's something else, a couple of computers perhaps, or a box of . . . maybe that's it. They don't know *what's* in it. It's like a Lucky Dip, a Christmas stocking, a bit of fun . . . a lottery.)

We have over half an hour to wait now, every word I write a lifetime in my heart. Several times I ask Matt if the violin is OK. Annoyed, he tells me to chill out. He's looking after it, isn't he? The men are moving now into their routine. (They have a routine. They've done this all before. I want to ask them: couldn't they find something else to steal, something lighter, smaller, easier to dispose of, something which wasn't going to cause so much pain? Do they know the pain that's coming around the corner toward me? Do I? Could I even envisage it? Maybe the loss that is coming my way is the only means through which I will understand what my violin truly means to me. Does it have to be that hard?)

Matt gets out his iPad. I rest my head against the pane of glass. There they are, where they always will be, behind us and to the side, ready to pounce. Only they don't pounce. They cause a diversion, two of them in front, one of them behind, the one behind, his arm snaking out. Here it is. One moment it's here, next to the luggage, quiet and safe, waiting for its next caress, the next . . . here it comes. I can't stop it now.

Matt looks up, asks me if I'm OK.

I say, "I feel really hot."

That's it. That's the last moment the old Min speaks, the Min who has lived with the violin since the age of six, who has practiced every day since the age of six, who has run the highs and the lows of her teenage years and who, at the age of twenty-one, found her soulmate, her lovely Stradivarius. Look at her, hot and tired and in a bit of a mood. What's she got to complain about? She has a record coming out, there are concerts lined up, there are plans, she still has a future. What's a cold or nausea or a bit of a mood in *that* scheme of things?

I raise my head. Suddenly it's got really crowded, people walking in, finding their seats, queuing at the counter. It had been so quiet up to that point. Something's different, I know, but I can't say what. It's like a shift in perspective, something out of kilter. The view looks the same, but there's something awry. What was it I was feeling? The action? The intent? And what prompted it? Had I noticed how the air had changed, how the space which was once a violin is now a violin no more? Was it my ankle, feeling the invisible strap of connection tugging out of reach? The eye, the heart, the breast; which part of me felt this unease? Which part sensed that I had been invaded, stolen, torn asunder, unstrung?

I look up at Matt and I say, "I have this really weird feeling that we've been had."

He looks down, says, a sudden rush to his voice, "Oh my God, where's your violin!"

"What do you mean, where's my violin?"

I stare down. There is the floor and the luggage, and there is his cello, but it's gone. We jump up, we look, we stare, we gasp for the sheer shock of it, my heart racing, my head bewildered. Voices are shouting. They could be mine, they could be Matt's, but it's screaming in my head. It's *gone*! It's *gone*!

I look around frantically, thinking I'm stupid, thinking I took it to the counter, thinking that we've missed it, that it's still there, pushed under the sea of cases, but it's gone! I can hear it in my head. I run to the exit, no one there, run back to the counter. I'm pelting the manager with questions. Did you see anything, someone's taken my case, did you see them? He thinks I've had a handbag snatched, tells me to calm down, it's no big deal. He doesn't understand. I ask him to call the police, but he still doesn't understand and he doesn't call the police, all the while, it's gone! It's gone . . .

Somebody tells me the transport police are stationed nearby and we run to find them, and I am yelling at Matt, "How could you? How could you?" And we find them and there's a young chap sitting there, and he doesn't understand either until I tell him it's worth a million pounds. It's a Stradivarius, I tell him, and it's my violin and it's gone! Voices ask me questions, what I saw, what happened and I answer them, my stomach clenched like it's been stabbed over and over again. Something is running out of me, something terrible, and there's a chasm yawning at my feet, without limit, and I am teetering on its edge. I want to run back to the time when it was safe, when I was whole. For it's coming on me now, that it's gone! It's gone! It's gone! But more than that . . .

I've gone too.

4

WELCOME TO LIMBOLAND.

At the beginning, the very beginning, at the British Transport Police station, all I could think about was, "What about my recording?" It was an odd thing to think about. It was safe enough, pressed and printed, ready to fly, yet, in those early hours, the question came back to me time and time again: "What about my recording?" And in the midst of it, as if by a weird form of telepathy, policemen coming and going, questions being asked, tea handed out, a message came through on my mobile from Sony, wanting some mundane stuff—times, addresses, etc.—and in a shot I'd tapped out, "Don't worry. Everything's fine." I didn't tell them that I was sitting in a police station, my world collapsing around me. I didn't tell them I was holding on so tight, fearful that if I ever let go I would . . . "No. Don't worry, Sony. Everything's fine!"

There was too much to take in. This could not be happening. How could it be? I had a violin. I had concerts to play, a recording contract to fulfill. It was Matt I was going to leave behind, not my violin. There was a young policeman there and I said to him, "If you slap me around the face, that will prove that this is a dream." He said, "I'm really sorry, ma'am, you're not dreaming. This is real."

Matt and I sat around in the police station for about four

hours, waiting to hear. The police were wonderful, right from the moment I stumbled up, panic-stricken. It wasn't every day a million-pound Stradivarius went missing on their patch, but they took the news in their stride, showed remarkable calm. At that point they were hopeful. The million aside, they'd seen this kind of thing before. There was always the possibility that this might have been some sort of scam on our part, but once they'd taken us out of the frame, they put out a red alert to all the train and Underground stations, hoping to catch them further down the line. With a spur-of-the-moment theft like that, nothing planned, it's hard to disappear. With a bit of luck, we were told, they'd be caught popping out of the ground somewhere. We waited there till well past midnight, hoping, hoping, hoping, but though the tea and sympathy were in full flow, the red alerts brought nothing, save some poor soul who had the misfortune to be traveling through King's Cross that night carrying his viola case. Brought in, case opened up, sent home. Lucky man; a hiccup in his life, a story to dine out on, perhaps a lesson of obsessive responsibility to learn: *Never let it go.*

We went home too, but after that first rush of optimism, drained and, more importantly, defeated. I think I knew by then that I'd lost. Somehow I'd lost. I didn't quite know the totality of what I had lost, couldn't quite bring myself to measure the depth and width of it, but I knew I'd lost, and knew too there were fathoms beneath me now, cold and dark. I could feel it creeping up on me, the numbness, gathering strength; chest, arms, head. I'd been thrown into unfamiliar waters, a big black ocean of them. I couldn't see it, but I knew it was out there, could sense it in all its unrelenting hugeness, its unimaginable strength, its terrible indifference to who and where I was. How could I live without my violin? What did this dark ocean know or care? It was an impossibility for me to envisage. My violin was going to stay with me until I died. That was the deal, the understanding between us. I'd be the one carried away in a box, not . . .

First, though, there was the wreckage to cling onto, threads of connection to the world that had left me behind. They were not pleasant chores, much like the practical issues that need to be sorted out after a death, and, like those, for a time they kept me level-headed and grounded. First thing the next morning I phoned Lark, the insurance company, and then I phoned Beare. I didn't phone my mother. I wasn't going to tell her. Maybe, I thought, it would all be over before she had to know. It would be like an unexpected medical scare—no need to let on until the news got really bad. That's what I told myself, but there were other reasons, which I can see only now. We were a self-contained unit, me and my violin. In a curious way, there was no person there to tell her that the violin had gone. That person wasn't fully formed yet, hadn't developed the power of speech. The former Min, the Min with the violin, wasn't used to telling my mother anything. Telling her things, being vulnerable, wounded, being a child, being an adolescent, being ordinary in that way, was not something I had ever done, not since I had been told of my destiny. When I'd had a cold, the worry for me hadn't been about me getting better, it had been about not being able to tackle the new piece I was meant to learn. Me plus the violin, that was the constant. I wasn't allowed to talk about my problems, show vulnerability, weakness, take the hits of adolescence. Put those needs away, Min! Take out your violin! My parents had an image of me that took breath without any discernible flaw—near-on perfect. And if I couldn't fulfill it, didn't fill that picture, couldn't breathe that air, what then . . .

So at the back of my mind there was a fear: if I let slip, she would start to flounder too, not knowing what to do, how to react, both of us lost. My violin had been the bridge between me and my family. We'd all walked to and fro across it to reach one another. Now that it had gone, what means did we have to reach one another? Only with it gone was the divide so plain to see. Standing apart, and now utterly alone, would inevitably bring me an ability to see things differently, to look at the life that had gone, in a different way.

It didn't matter anyway. Someone at Beare had phoned home to commiserate, not realizing my intention. My mother rang me immediately, of course she rang, stunned, not quite believing—for how many times in the last ten years had she ever seen me *without* my violin? Straight off I told her what I had always told her: that I was fine, that everything would be OK, even though I knew it wouldn't be, already wasn't. Everything fine was being carried away on that implacable sea. But for her, for her-and-me, it was the lifeboat I'd just clambered aboard, the *Everything Fine*.

About a day later I got a call from the police, from DI Andy Rose. They knew a lot more now. They'd seen the CCTV footage, recognized the thieves immediately, knew exactly who they were. They came from the traveling community, two teenage brothers, quite young, and an older uncle: an extended family. Although the police were a couple of days behind, it would just be a matter of pinning them down, finding the violin. They knew what was likely to have happened. At some level they knew exactly what had happened. They'd traced the three of them from Tottenham, where they all lived, to pitching up at Euston and coming out of the tube. They'd followed the film as the trio moved into the food court, slipping in and out, before going into Pret. Scavengers, that's what they were, sharp eyes, ready beaks and claws, feeding on opportunity. They'd sat and watched the footage as the boys spotted the case, made their collective move, brought the case under their influence; no finesse apparently, no Fagin-like skill on display, as I had imagined, just a no-nonsense easing-out of the case and then, up, up and away, out of the rear exit, which, fortuitously, was about to be closed. (This, at least, is what I have been told happened. Five years on and I still can't bring myself to watch it. In a moment of clear perception and understanding, Andy suggested that I keep a copy of the film so that *should* I want to look at it, I will always have the means—that in that sense it won't be a forbidden fruit, something denied me; that I could keep it in a box, slip it into a machine, hold my breath and press Play. But I can't imagine that I ever would wish to see it. What would it do? Absolve me, deepen my sense of guilt, of anger? And, that aside, who would want to watch a recording of something so upsetting? I never took him up on the offer.)

Enough. Mission accomplished, the thieves then disappeared for a time, on a bus it's presumed, for they then reappeared in the High Road in Tottenham, just down from the police station, where of course they were known, but in this instance, as yet, were not. On the bus, it's clear that they have taken the violin out of its case, and cottoned on to the fact that it's a Stradivarius (it says so on the inside of the violin), for what they did next was to go into an internet café, log in and Google-up, checking out what a Stradivarius might be. It's clear they didn't quite realize what they had.

If I think about the thieves at all, it is around this time, when they first opened the case up at the back of the bus, lifted it out. Did it glow for them like it glows for me? Did they pluck at its strings, did they *hear* it, how the notes blossomed inside? Didn't it sing to them, melt their rough, scavenging hearts? No, apparently not, for there was a bus driver there in the café too, and in this state of not-knowing, or possibly not believing what the screen was telling them, they turned to this man and offered the violin to him, would have handed it over for a clutch of fivers, fifteen/twenty quid, not even a hundred, no sweat. And the bus driver thought about it, and came to the conclusion that he didn't need one of those, and knocked the offer back. And then, back on the screen perhaps, Google would have insisted that they wise up. They had lifted a Stradivarius, one of only 449 in the whole wide world. Maybe they'd have believed it, maybe they wouldn't. They didn't offer it to anyone else. They went home, just up the road, wondering what they should do. Curse or blessing? The family would know.

The police visited the house, confronted the father of the two brothers with what they had stolen. He was wary, suspicious, the boys long gone, the violin who knew where? Andy told me that the best way to recover the violin would be to go to the press, let the thieves know what they'd got, give the message out loud and clear that, if they played it right, everyone could come out of this OK. It was the obvious thing to do. It was a good story, with a real hook—the ex-child prodigy and her million-pound violin. A story like that would feature in all the newspapers, broadsheets, tabloids, could even make the front page. The thieves had to be told things, had to know that what they had done was real and serious, had to know how valuable it was, had to understand that the police's prime concern was not feeling their collars, but getting the violin back. They wouldn't trust the police delivering such a message, but they might trust the press. Intelligence, knowledge, a feel for the world my violin now inhabited were coming into play. The act of theft and the follow-through had quickly morphed from the simple act of catching them and restoring the violin to its rightful owner into what would be a long-drawn-out battle of wits; a matter of guile and patience. The decision had been made, and it was one that the police would keep to. It would be good to get the lads behind this, but it's better to get the violin.

Publicity, that's what the police needed—but I shrank from the idea, terrified. Publicity was a shark circling me, hungry for blood. There were wounds I'd have to endure, pain. I just couldn't deal with it. No publicity. As always, Andy and Tony (the young police officer who was first on the scene) were hugely understanding. They told me not to worry, we'll do it without your help; keep your name, your identity, out of it. The Strad should be enough. You can remain anonymous. They put out a press release: the violin, its value, where it was stolen, the date, the time. What we hadn't thought through was the fact that my violin was only one of two Strads made in 1696. So the press did their research, found an old interview I'd done, and worked out that I was the celebrated fool—all in a matter of hours. They rang the police, told them what they'd found, informed them that they were running with the story whether we confirmed it or not. We confirmed it, no choice in the matter.

I'd never dealt with this sort of press before—had been brought up on a diet of tame interviews, prodigies to patronize, concerts to be given, records to be released, that sort of fodder. This was a different matter, a more feral breed of press, quicker, wilder, more intent on its survival, there to suck the story clean to its bones. Maybe I should have given myself over to a proper interview, attempted to steer the story my way, talked over their heads to the thieves direct. Maybe if I'd done something then they wouldn't have reported that I'd left my violin lying unattended for half an hour, that on that cold November night, at approximately 8:30 p.m., Euston station had witnessed the purchase of the world's most expensive sandwich. It was a joke to them, and I the idiot. You could imagine commuters on the train, reading the story as the stations slipped by, sharing the joke, *Have you heard this one?* To me, unable to reply, it was simply unkind, a low and unnecessary blow to a body already battered, the accusation painful like a knocked bruise. What had I ever done to them? To a sympathetic outsider, the worst they might think was that it made me look ridiculous, irresponsible, but to me it made me sound as if I had been a bad mother to my violin, as if I was responsible for the damage I had caused it. And, of course, that was the trouble. I was.

The press weren't the only ones. There were so many comments and criticisms made by people who couldn't understand why I didn't have a bodyguard—incredulity that I'd been traveling with a million-pound Stradivarius *on public transport*. What they failed to realize is that that's how everyone travels with their instruments. No bodyguards, no chauffeur-driven, bulletproof cars, just planes and boats and trains. I didn't respond. Again, should I have done? Come out fighting, told my side of the story? Hard to say, though evidence suggests that entering into that arena never seems to do anyone any good. The story isn't there for you. If you fight it, you'll be fighting a battle you can't win, and which the story doesn't want you to win. The story has its own agenda, its own rules, its own purpose. It's like a review. You can't reply. Even the act of replying only serves to heighten the color of your faults further. Matt was nervous too, worried that he was going to be blamed, afraid that what had happened at Pret would come out.

The publicity seemed endless. I felt as if I were being buried under a great weight of unwanted attention. It was almost a physical thing, pressing down on me. I began to have visions of a demon squatting on my chest, pressing down on my lungs, suffocating me. He had more than a spirit. He had form. He dug into me. I tried to ward him off. I cut my near-waist-length hair to a severe chin-length bob. I wore deliberately plain clothes, reducing myself to a minimum. Black. The not-getting-it-back was taking hold, that numbness very nearly total. There was a pain inside me, but there was this long deadness too, as if my body were producing its own supply of Grade A morphine, Min there but not there, awake but barely conscious, in pain but not at all. Min the fast-emptying shell. Sometimes I tried filling the shell, filling it with imagined, ill-constructed feeling. I would start to shake, as if my body were trying to grab me by the shoulders, wake me up out of it. But there was little or nothing to wake.

It was very cold outside; the bitter winter settled in. No warmth without, no warmth within. I stayed in bed most days and when I was finally able to get up, all I wanted was to go back to bed again and dream of my violin. If I couldn't see it, or touch it, at least I could dream about it. Dreams were my reality. They weren't good dreams, but my violin was there, sometimes before me, sometimes not. I would dream that it was buried in a garden; I would dream that it was cold like me, wrapped up, half suffocated, alone. Other times, my dream would place me on a train and my violin was on the tracks, defenseless before the wheels. Or I'd be on a train sitting by the window, half content, and I'd see it on the platform, abandoned. Other times it would be the violin on the train and me on the platform. Either way, I'd get a glimpse of it and suddenly the train would move, and I, or my violin, would glide away, and the dream would start again. There it is! And then it wouldn't be—always out of reach. Not good, except for one thing. I always dreamt it intact, never dreamt it burned or disfigured or destroyed. Not once. Not in my darkest days did I ever dream that.

I started to think of alternatives, and ideas of childhood came back. Long ago, when my first violin had appeared, I'd also dreamt of being a ballerina. I loved ballet and was quite good at it. My teacher had thought so too, told me that I should be a dancer, but my mother was resolutely against it, made me give it up. Too much hard work, she said (and the violin wasn't?), but that wasn't the only reason. I think there was a prejudice against it, to lead a dancer's life, and all the connotations it brought. I'd loved it. Dancing had been relatively pressure-free. I didn't have to be anyone else. I was a little girl dancing. Just to write those four words now brings back a taste of lost times. A little girl dancing. Then dancing was no more. A little girl not dancing. A little girl fenced off, secured, not really a little girl anymore. A little something else. We all know what. At the time I'd been terribly upset, and then the violin had taken over, and there were no hours in the day for dancing anyway. I forgot about it, forgot about the little girl I could have been, should have been, forgot about a lot of things.

Well, it was too late for me to become a ballerina, but a doctor? I had a friend who'd done exactly that, worked in the London Sinfonietta, given it up, retrained as a doctor, was now a GP. It sounded sensible, attractive, my feet on grounded earth. I could imagine myself in my surgery, pressing the buzzer, waiting for the next patient, smiling as they walked into the room. I'd be helping people. I'd have a goal, be fulfilled. I wouldn't be empty anymore. I looked into courses. Without a degree, it would take me seven years, but with a degree under my belt I could have fast-tracked in two. Two years and I'd be a junior doctor. I looked into volunteering at a hospital, had a serious talk about it with my friend. She warned me about the hardships, about the tough hours. That wouldn't put me off. I could do tough hours. What else could I do?

I got back into yoga, practiced religiously. It was a way of removing myself from the pain, but also offered me another view of things. My yoga teacher encouraged me to think of training, move into teaching. I didn't have to be hard-core, she told me. There would be many different levels open to me. *Open to me.* There was a strange thought. It didn't seem quite possible, engaging in that way, but it told me something unexpected: both inclinations/suggestions came with the tag of interaction attached, that there was a person lurking somewhere inside me that didn't need a violin to communicate with people, that I *did* have a voice, that there was a me outside the violin. An extraordinary thought.

But I still wanted it back. I did something else, something that I kept very quiet about at the time. I went to a psychic, or rather I stumbled across one. I was in Selfridges, buying a card. The stationery section is in the basement, and I noticed this purple curtain hanging down at one end. Curious, I poked my head around it, and there was this cubbyhole, and a big sign that read "Psychic Sisters." I'd probably walked past this heaven knows how many times before, but this was the first time I'd noticed it. That seemed to me to have some relevance. I went in. Psychic Sisters is run by a woman called Jayne. She's not always there. She hires the place out and then hires her psychic sisters to come in and do their stuff. But this time the big psychic sister herself was there in person.

She said, "You've had your heart broken, haven't you?"

"Yes, but probably not in the way you think."

I told her I'd had something taken from me, an object.

"Somebody stole something very valuable to you."

"Yeah."

"A boy with curly hair has buried it in a garden."

Well, that was news of sorts. And one of the boys in the footage *did* have curly hair. And I'd already dreamt about a garden. I went to see her three times, never told her it was a violin that had done the damage. Every time I left she'd say, "Don't lose hope. Good things are going to start happening again," and sometime before that, would announce, as if it mattered to her, "It's such a waste of your talents." What did she think my talents were? How did she know I had any? I never gave her my name, never told her my story. Was it crazy to go there or simply a sign of desperation? I believed in signs, in feelings, had them myself. I believed I could hear my violin, believed we were still connected. Was it so impossible to imagine that the waves out there might not be picked up by Jayne and her psychic sisters? (Later, writing this book,

I made this embarrassing confession to Simon Taylor of the transport police. He looked amused and understanding. They consult psychics all the time!)

Matt persuaded me to give up my flat in London and stay with him in Manchester. Much of the time was occupied preparing him for the next stage in his career. His final exams were coming up, and understandably they came first. We both focused our energies on getting him polished and ready. It was good for me too, kept me occupied. No yoga lessons, no medical texts to haul around, but helping him as best I could. I would sit in on his cello lessons, listen to him practice, accompany him to auditions. Once we flew out to New York using my air miles so that he could attend an audition there. I wanted to support him. As a mature student it was vital that he didn't delay his development any further. We went down once to visit his parents (not mine). They were worried about Matt's liability with regard to the theft. I assured them that nothing would happen on that score, resolved to take his lead. I wanted to disappear, to run away from my life. What *was* my life? What was my career?

Matt fielded all my calls, friends as well as business, told them that I wasn't ready to talk. He backed me in not talking to my parents, told me that it would only upset them to see me in such a state. I couldn't disagree with that. So, weeks in, they still had no idea of the state I was in. Nothing new there. When I tell my mother about it now, she says, "I wish you'd told me," and I say, "I wish it too." So *what* if she'd been upset? That's what mothers are for, to get upset, to give you comfort. And when we talk about it now, we get upset together, a little late in the day, but very welcome for all that, for both of us.

Matt encouraged me in my bad habits. Close to my family, but not close. When I managed to speak to friends, they begged me to come back down, nearer to people and places I knew. One in particular didn't think it was a good idea for me to stay up in Manchester, alone and dependent on one man, a man whom I'd already tried to leave. This friend had three daughters, all just younger than me. "You need to be with people you know," he would say, "people you have known a long time, people you can trust." But I didn't. Although I knew I'd have to leave him eventually, I needed Matt. Matt was the one who'd lived through this, who was a part of the Min that was left behind. For heaven's sake, he'd been the last one to handle the violin case! *That* was the connection I couldn't break from, and for Matt too, that night in Euston station had given him a place in the world, a set of events and emotions in which he was the fulcrum.

So, not surprisingly, Matt—who appeared alarmed at the idea that one day I *would* leave—did everything he could to dissuade me from going away without him, even for the shortest of times. Who knew what would happen, how my head might turn, away from his influence? Also, he was nervous about the possibility of getting caught in the firing line himself, and I couldn't blame him for not wanting that.

Gradually I gave him more and more control over me. Anything I did had to be run by him and he was happy to step up to the plate. Once, when I prepared lunch for myself, he cooked it all again, because I hadn't cooked it right. I was back in Euston station, being corrected on how I was sitting, and didn't even notice. (And putting that down now, I am reminded of my childhood, the diktat of how we would eat at home. And there I was, twenty-five years later, being told how to eat again. Mealtimes: who cooks them, who eats them, immutable measure of control.) There were times when he tried to jolly me along, encouraged me to go out and engage in "fun" activities; others when it seemed he was reluctant for me to even leave the flat. I would end up locking myself in the spare bedroom just to get away from the noise—my head, his presence; it was hard to distinguish which was which. One day, coming back into the flat, feeling low and despondent, making for the spiral staircase in the lobby, the air still and quiet and calm, a figure sprang out from under the darkened stairwell, bellowing in my ear.

"Boo!"

Arms wrapped around me. It was Matt playing a prank. He wrapped his arms around me, thought it a great joke. I thought I'd been attacked. Still do.

He could read me. Keep up appearances, he said, homing in on something that is so important to Korean culture. He'd had those Korean girlfriends before. He understood our way of thinking, our values, knew what to say, how to say it. Because, that whole dread time, I never wanted people to know how low I was, would go to extreme lengths to hide it. I could lie in bed all day, all week if need be, but if I had a meeting, the underwriter up from London, say, I would gather up my energies, step out of the door all prepped up, keeping face. But while I am Korean, I am English too, and keeping up those sorts of appearances took its toll. It accentuated the disconnect my life was taking, the four walls of the flat and the world outside. All I wanted was my lost sanity, but I had no idea how to find it. I just wanted to be left in silence, alone with my thoughts. Trying to reconnect with what senses I had left.

November, December, January—elongated stretches of nothing. What did I do, what did I think, who was the Min there, inhabiting this body? It wasn't the old one, and it isn't the one here right now, but it was there, in form, in shape. You could touch it, speak to it, hear it respond, but what it thought it was is hard to say. Beare lent me a violin, a Bergonzi. I opened up the case, took one look at it, shut the lid, locked it back up. I didn't open it again for weeks, couldn't look at it, just couldn't. It sat on a chair, dominating the room like a perfect little coffin, as if a little someone had died in that room, as if I were the body's caretaker. I was living alongside something that had passed away. I would look at the case and imagine my own violin, where it was, what was happening to it. Was it still in its case, and where was the case? Dreams were merging into daylight thought. Was it lying propped up, somewhere cold, an outhouse, a garage, some rickety back shelf? Perhaps it was being jolted up and down, traveling in the back of a van, on its way to change hands in a field, a car park. Wherever it was, it was outside the law, outside its social milieu. It wouldn't know how to behave, wouldn't know the rules of accepted engagement.

Was it alone? Did it miss me? How strange that looks to write, "Did it miss me?," and yet I knew it to be true. The violin was part of me, and I part of the violin. It was as simple and as helpless as that. The violin had made me whole, the only thing, and I, in turn, had reciprocated. Of course it missed me! It still does. But that box on the chair? It had something desiccated inside, that was all, or if not dead then something *alien*, a threat to my shut-down safety. A little later

Beare offered me another violin, a real beauty of a Guarneri del Gesù, even rarer than my own dear Strad, but it was no use. It wasn't *my* violin. Someone at Beare, meaning to be kind, said, "Yours is not the only violin in the world, Min," to which I said nothing, but to which I should have replied, "But it is to me." If it had been my child that had been stolen, would people have expected me to accept *another* one? Just as good!

Sony was as sympathetic as they could be. "Do what you need to do," they said. "We can put it all on hold." They were acting as my agents then, and I could barely communicate with them. What normally happens is a CD is released initially in one country and then you have a series of staggered releases over the year in others. Different releases, different concerts following different interviews, your CD rolled out across the globe. That's how it had worked for the Beethoven and that's how it had been planned for the Brahms, only on a larger, more intensive scale. Not this time.

The decline was not immediate. It happened in stages. At the start I told myself, "Whatever happens, I have to do this. I am a professional." My whole life I've been taught how to be a professional. If you're ill, too bad, you have to play. (The only time I had ever canceled a concert was when I had come down with pneumonia. There had been two back-to-back concerts, one in Hexham on the Wednesday, then Thursday in Darlington. Halfway through the first concert I had a bad attack of asthma, wheezing and coughing away, not a good foil for the pianist at all. Afterward he told me that playing the next night was out of the question. He took me to the hospital instead and there I was told I had pneumonia.) So to begin with, the training stepped in, the reflex action of a player who is thinking in terms of performing, even though every fiber of her being is telling her that it's impossible. I told them I'd be all right, but I couldn't play the Brahms. It was just too close to what had happened, to what my violin meant to me. I'd play the Mendelssohn instead, or possibly the Beethoven. But then, when I thought about it—if thinking is the right word—I realized I couldn't do that either. I was empty-handed, nothing to fill them with. What would I be holding? What sound was going to come out? Mine? How would that be possible? There would be a stranger in my arms—how could I let it speak for me? Each time a date came up I turned away. I couldn't do it. Sony did their patient best, but they're a commercial company and there came a point when the marketing people said, "We have to go ahead with the release."

Music was trying to drag me back, but before Sony made the decision, those first few months I couldn't even listen to it. Music had been my life, as full of nourishment as the blood in my veins, the air in my lungs, but right then I felt as if I'd been emptied of it all. Bed was all. OK, I got up every now and again, answered calls, sounded (sometimes) almost human, but mainly it was the bed, my two cats, Billy and Lilly, my only comfort. Not wishing to emerge, to surface, might have appeared as if I was excusing myself from life, but it wasn't quite like that. I was suspended, held in a safe, silent fluid, waiting for the moment for the eyelid to flutter, the muscle to twitch, to feel that flicker of life start within me. I hadn't given up. I'd shut down. There's a difference. Babies shut down when they're very ill, everything suspended in order to preserve what little they have. Most animals do it too. They're not checking out: quite the reverse, they're trying to stay alive, waiting for the time when it's safe to stir again, when they're strong enough, feel they can face the outside. That's how I stayed for those early months, the second time in my life that I'd done that. The first was after my love affair with Robert ended. My violin got me out. The second was now. My violin had got me in. I couldn't imagine a third.

Was it the end of the first month that music nudged me awake, or the beginning of the second? I can't remember, can't recall the prompt. Blood or breath, I began to need it again, to reassure myself that I was alive. I started listening to some Bach. It was the right place to start. For me music always begins and ends with Bach, everything stripped down to the purity of the note. After Bach came Schubert. I took great comfort in him, his string quartets (*Rosamunde*, *Death and the Maiden*) and the achingly beautiful quintet (one of the last works he composed). After Schubert came Fauré. Without quite knowing it I was pointing myself in the direction I would be able to take. Fauré's two piano quartets are a perfect example of an artist's development. They were composed only seven years apart but listen to them side by side and they seem almost from different composers; the lightness of engagement of the first replaced with the final turbulent rush into the unknown of the second, the music composed almost without bar lines, held out just beyond your grasp. Piano quartets, violin sonatas, they were reaching out toward me, stretching beyond their lines, beyond confinement. That was it. Music was starting to show me the way out, beyond my confinement. Small wonder then that it was Bach and Schubert and Fauré who made me look at that box sitting on the table and the Bergonzi silent inside.

Matt was out. I was on my own, in the front room of his

flat. The flat was a converted law chambers; the window looked down onto the street, across to rooms that were still offices, people inside, typing, answering phones, getting on with their lives. It was a working environment. I opened up the case, picked up the Bergonzi. The first thing you do on a new instrument is to play the open strings, get a feel for the vibrations lying in it, get the measure of the body of the instrument, to see how it responds, discover what it responds to. I played the open strings, then some slow scales. It felt like a hollow box. *I* felt like a hollow box. After ten years of playing on one instrument, knowing my way around every millimeter, the Bergonzi had a completely different navigation, the distances between the notes unfamiliar, the response to the bow different. I was using my old student bow, good enough for when I was sixteen, but in that room it felt as if I were holding a stranger, trying to break the ice with a golf club. The sound the Bergonzi made wasn't unpleasant but, if it had a core, I couldn't get to the heart of it, couldn't hear its soul. I knew I was being unfair. It was a Bergonzi. It had a heart, it had a soul, but there was resentment in my arm. Even the look of it set me on edge. How dare it try to replace my violin, my affections!

I ran some scales, and then played a D-minor chord, marking the opening of Bach's Chaconne. The Chaconne is the final part of Bach's Partita No. 2. He composed it around 1720, after returning from a trip to find that his wife had died. The Chaconne, in essence a series of variations on a single theme, is a work of extraordinary intensity. In a letter to Clara Schumann, Brahms called it one of the most wonderful, incomprehensible pieces of music, and went on: "On one stave, for a small instrument, the man writes a whole world of the deepest thoughts and most powerful feelings. If I imagined that I could have created, even conceived the piece, I am quite certain that the excess of excitement and earth-shattering experience would have driven me out of my mind." But Bach was not a romantic like Brahms, and if he was composing for anyone it was not for a person, or the memory of them, it was to the glory of God. That in part explains the complex single-mindedness of all Bach—God was his ultimate audience. For the solo player the Chaconne is one of the longest and most challenging of pieces ever written, and yet, the simplicity of its intent, its astonishing grace and beauty, are one of the great summits of human achievement, a peak of purity that one longs to climb. It is everything good about being human.

So in that room, alone, traffic and people outside, not to mention the world, I became human again. I played the Chaconne, and as I played it I could feel the spirit of its music reconnecting with part of my brain, part of my body. I was playing Bach, and Bach was playing me. Bach was reaching out to me, and I felt his touch. And there was the other matter that I'd forgotten. The thing about being a violinist (or perhaps any other player—gymnast, painter, ballet dancer) is that there's a part of you that *is* the instrument, and you have to feed that part on a regular basis. It demands to be fed. You wake up and it tells you that it is hungry. It needs food. So I began feeding it again, the bare minimum to start with, playing once or twice a week, but keeping it alive. I was keeping my fingers warmed up, getting the muscle memory going again. I was still staying in bed all day, still rousing myself to meet those I had to, still putting on an appearance when I thought it necessary—all part of the performer's instinct of stepping up to the performing plate. And some of it took some play-acting too.

Once, out shopping at Tesco, I took a call from the loss adjuster. The line was bad, I moved into a little alleyway so I could block the noise, wishing I was at home to take this call. And it was a bad call. A couple of dealers he'd spoken to had told him that my violin had been vastly underinsured. It was worth a lot more than the policy covered. This could be catastrophic. Another stab to the stomach. I scurried home, riffled through the contract. There it lay, the clause I feared. To understand why, I need to show you a simple sum. Say an instrument is insured for £1,000 but is in fact valued at £1,500. When it comes to an insurance claim, before an insurance company will pay out the insurance sum, the owner has to pay the difference, i.e. £500. In this case it would have run to tens of thousands of pounds, perhaps hundreds of thousands of pounds. It could have been the end. Luckily Beare stood by their original valuation of £750,000, but it reminded me what a world of shifting sand dealership is. For many of them the violins are all. Players are an unnecessary nuisance. Players get in the way of value, what the violin is worth. (That, after all, is why Stradivari made them. To up the price, five hundred years later.) The contract stood firm. The violin had not been found within the six-month stipulation, and so the money was paid out. Relief, but no joy at all. It had all the allure of a deathbed bequest.

But at least I was playing again. And playing was a form of escapism too; it was leading me back in but also leading away from the reality that could fall dead on my shoulders and send me, slumped, back to bed. It was doing two contradictory things: setting me free, keeping me grounded. Music hath alarms, indeed.

The Brahms was released, three months late. Funnily enough, though I barely had anything to do with it I was excited about it. Sony had breathed on the dying embers of my previous life and for a moment they flickered back into life. Brought back the tears too. This was supposed to be my time. Everything should have been happening to me now. My record was out. I should have been giving interviews, been making myself ready for a world waiting to receive me. There was a stage out there. There were hundreds of them, stretching out into the distance, stages that I'd been preparing for all my life! I should have been feeling a flurry of wild trepidation, nervous excitement, a grounded confidence too, seeing how close it all was, how very close, that all I needed to do was to walk out, take my stand, lift my bow and . . . But I was stuck in Manchester. Nothing was happening there.

It all went wrong. My contract was with Sony Korea, so other territories would have to buy the rights from them. The plan was, once it had been released and found its feet, those other territories would follow. But there had been no concerts, no publicity, so the Korean sales were minimal. And it's a brutal industry. Who was going to be interested in buying a license from which they'd get no revenue? Even with iTunes, though it's easy to put something out, if an album is not deemed to be one of their front-line products, forget it. I'd missed my original deadline, the allocated slot for my CD didn't get the profile. I felt unprofessional. Sony might have recognized that I didn't do this deliberately, but I knew how the recording world worked. My record was a record of tragedy. I'd worked for this moment for the past two years. It was my second album, much better than anything I'd recorded before. But in the end it made its appearance like a badly placed firework on a damp November evening. It flew up, it fluttered into brief, unremarkable life, sank back to the ground. I'd missed my chance. It wouldn't come back.

I voiced these concerns to Matt. He set up a Facebook and Twitter page for me, a way, he suggested, of reconnecting. I took it as an act of encouragement but soon regretted it. On his insistence (yes, that word again), and after initial resistance, I gave him all my passwords. He'd manage my messages. That was fine by me. I didn't want to have anything to do with it. I was regularly receiving abusive messages from online trolls and Matt would show me what was doing the rounds. I guess he was trying to be supportive, but it only seemed to add to the idea that the world outside ran on hurt.

He was starting to distance himself from what had happened, his part in it. He was anxious to be a part of the debacle, would use it as an ice-breaker in conversation, but in this version of events there was a distance between the table and the chairs and the violin in his care. Here, I became the one where the dark shadows fell, who let it go (and he was right about that, that was the trouble, I *did* let it go), while he stood in the sunlight. What amazes me now is that I never confronted it properly, never took the stand. Why would that be? Was I so weak, my mind so removed from any sense of ownership, that it didn't matter? Or was it more to do with the fact that he was a man, and that I was Min, trained to accept the reality that all the men who had guided and taught me had insisted *was* the reality? There was a determination here, his determination, that outwitted mine. Like the times before, there were occasions when I had moments of clarity, when I could see this was not a relationship I wanted to be in, but I didn't have the energy to match Matt's will. His exams were coming up. How unfair would that be if I left him in the lurch at such a critical moment? Besides, he would say, I wasn't seeing straight. That was true.

Although I had canceled all the major concerts, there was still one I hadn't dustbinned—set for June, the day of my birthday. I was supposed to play in Oxford, and now as I was playing again, albeit spasmodically, I kept on thinking, "Shall I do it, can I do it?" I didn't know how it would pan out, or what it would pan out to, but I couldn't have a violin case staring at me accusingly any longer. I had to get another violin—not as a replacement, but instead like the fitting of an artificial limb (you'd rather have your old leg back, but if you can't, let's see how you walk with this one). But which? From whom? How much? I didn't know if my violin was ever going to be recovered, did I? I didn't have a career. I didn't have an income.

And how was I possibly going to afford the maintenance? That's another subject I haven't gone into. With violins like my Strad or the Guadagnini that might have been, you don't simply buy them, stick them in a case, rub some rosin on the bow every now and again and hope for the best. These are high-maintenance creatures. They need constant care and attention, and the cash to do it. They need to be indulged. Every whim, every wish, every hint of a blemish and off you go to the luthier. Maybe the bridge doesn't suit—maybe you need to spend money on another bow (a really good bow starts at about £50,000). A violin like mine costs around £5,000 a year on upkeep. How was I going to afford such an instrument?

Personal matters that I had attended to had devoured a good part of the insurance money, on top of my living expenses and tax bills. After the violin was stolen, my parents had been going through a hard time too. They had bought their house back in 2000 when their business was going well, but then, when September 11 happened, it folded overnight. They were approaching retirement age and there was simply not enough coming in. They were hemorrhaging cash. Their only way out was to sell their house, or see it repossessed. And I had the remainder of my insurance money sitting in the bank. Yes, I knew what it meant, what the consequences might be, but what else was I to do? They didn't like it. They were Korean, it assaulted their very core, but there was no way I was going to allow my parents' house to be repossessed. So I loaned them the money they needed. They still have their home, where they should be.

Matt found this violin Tarisio had in New York, a Strad. He had phoned Jason Price the week after my violin was stolen, had asked him if there were any suitable ones coming up on the market. Jason had told him about the Castelbarco. It was a known instrument. Charles Beare had had it in his vault for any number of years. When the current owners decided to sell the violin, Tarisio stepped in, offering to sell it for them. It had been one of a quartet of Strads that had been commissioned by Castelbarco back in the 1700s. It was originally a far superior instrument to my violin, one of the top four that Stradivari ever made—the Viotti Strad, the Messiah, the Lady Blunt and this—the backs all made from one glorious piece of maple. No one knows what happened to it, but unfortunately—and this happened to any number of instruments—it had probably been kept in a soft case, and the bridge had smashed into the body, causing substantial damage. (Damage would often define the history of these unlucky instruments—there are stories of top violins and cellos being used in marching bands.) The damage had been severe. The original top was missing; it had a French top and an Italian back. (It was Charles Beare who discovered that it had a French top, years back. The then-owners demanded an apology, insisted that he was wrong, that it was an unadulterated thoroughbred, but now it's clear to everyone.) In mint condition it would have been worth around five million dollars, but because of the wars it had been through, it was within my reach. I wasn't at all sure that it would be the right violin for me, wasn't even capable of thinking about such things, but I had to face up to the fact that it would be nigh-on impossible to find another Strad that was in better condition at a price I could handle. There was no harm in having a look. I arranged to meet Jason when he was next in London.

Matt and I met him at a Mayfair hotel bar. He was tall, elegant, with a slightly long, angular face, thin lips. He'd been down at Prussia Cove, but we hadn't met then. Was it this time that he was in one of his perfectly fitting suits, or was he dressed down in designer jeans? Can't remember. Whenever we did meet he was always impeccable. We ordered a bottle of water.

"I am so sorry, Min," Jason said. "It must be a terrible time for you."

I thanked him. There was no use in pretending otherwise. He was sympathetic, understanding.

"We had the fax that's being circulated to all the dealers," he told me. "I couldn't believe it when Matt called and said it was your violin. How much do the police know?"

I told him as much as I could. But that wasn't all. I was getting upset.

"It's being reported in the press that I was careless and left my violin unattended," I said. "I wasn't careless. The violin . . ."

Matt steamed in. No, it wasn't carelessness. They were professional thieves, and the violin was right near her . . . Hang on. Was I hearing this right? The violin was *where* exactly? Matt was changing course.

"So, I've been telling Min about the Castelbarco you have coming up in the next auction."

Jason nodded. "Yes, we have this wonderful . . ." His words washed over me. I was looking at Matt, Matt was looking at Jason, Jason was looking at me. The violin was *next* to me? I wanted to rein it all in, bring the conversation back to the theft, back to Pret and the argument and Matt on his wretched iPad, but I couldn't. It would be too awkward. I'd only just met the guy. So, yes, the Castelbarco sounded interesting.

"Of course," he said, and I picked up on this bit, "if you got your old violin back and you needed to sell this, we would help with that." That was good to hear. So, yes, I should take a look, yes, it was nice to meet you, Jason Price.

Later though, I confronted Matt, asked him why on earth he'd said that, fudged the issue.

"I was trying to protect your privacy," he explained. "It's such a complicated thing, explaining to people what happened. I thought I was helping you out. I'm sorry if I got that wrong."

He was sorry. I let it go. Writing that makes me feel like such a fool. I let it go. Why didn't I challenge him? Was it exhaustion, incipient depression or just the weight of Matt upon me, constricting my thoughts and actions?

We flew to New York two days before the auction. Tarisio's offices were around the corner from Carnegie Hall. We took the lift to the right floor, were greeted by the receptionist, who showed us to the showroom where the Castelbarco lay among a dozen other violins. I lifted it up, ran a bow across its strings. Unmistakable. A thrill shivered up my arms, the room filled with that special sound. It wasn't my violin, but it was a Strad. It had a real quality to it that shone through its composite drawbacks (and you could tell they were there, difficulties in expression lying in wait). But I had great sympathy for it, its mysterious past, its somewhat forlorn appearance.

The next day I went to see it again, played it again but not for long. In auctions you aren't allowed that luxury. And again the following day. It was pulling at me and I couldn't decide. Come the auction day and I still wasn't convinced. I told Matt that I thought I should call Beare, ask their advice. He didn't warm to that idea at all. I liked the violin. It would be a huge mistake not to buy it.

"What do you need to call them for?" he said. "They'll only try and talk you out of it. They're not going to want you to buy a violin from another dealer, are they?"

He had a point. Nevertheless, I rang Beare, talked to Steven. He advised me not to buy it. The best thing I could do would be to buy a Guadagnini, an Italian violin maker widely considered to be the third-greatest violin maker after Stradivari and Giuseppe Guarneri. It would not only be a top violin suited to my temperament and style, it would also be a good investment should my own violin ever be recovered. There wouldn't be any problem in selling a Guadagnini, and thereby raising enough money for the recovered Strad. If it took years to find, so much the better! There was only one way the value of a good Guadagnini was going, and that was up.

It was convincing. I rang Jason, told him I was pulling out of the auction, explained the reasons. He was horrified, his anger barely suppressed.

"I don't think Beare has your best interests at heart," he said. "It's precisely the kind of thing a rival dealer would say to try and kill a sale. If getting the money back quickly is the issue, that's not a problem." His voice softened. "Look, there's still a bit of time before the auction ends, why don't you and Matt take a walk, discuss it between you? You can come back and make a bid right here in the office, if that's what you want to do."

We left, took a long walk around Manhattan. I was still of the mind not to bid. Beare had always been good to me. Matt was furious.

"Don't listen to them. If he cared that much about helping you he would have already done it by now. He's a businessman and if you buy this violin, he knows he's lost a client. Of course he's going to try and put you off. Frankly, if he cared enough he'd have been more active in his search straightaway. Jason is a friend. He sympathizes. It's a relationship based on trust."

Round and round we went. He was right. At least I'd have a violin that I could call my own. At least it would be a step in the right direction. I was fed up with Limboland. But I wasn't going to go in all guns blazing. I'd place one low bid, leave it at that, see if the Strad needed me to the same degree as I needed it. We went back to Tarisio's with just a few minutes to spare. I placed my bid at £250,000, way below the estimate, the whole office on tenterhooks. I could feel them rooting for me.

"Let's pull the plug, so no one else can bid!" someone joked.

5, 4, 3, 2, 1 . . . the Strad was mine.

It was a strange moment, a mixture of relief, happiness, slightly disorienting too. I had reentered the real world, wasn't sure quite what I'd do in it.

We flew back. I was pleased, relieved. Life wasn't back on the rails exactly, but I had made a commitment to something other than loss. Perhaps this violin meant I was moving in the right direction. But Matt's attitude was peculiar. For him, me buying the violin seemed like an entry for him, a sort of validation of who he was. It wasn't the fact that I'd got another violin that pleased him, it was the deal, the mechanics, the money. He was excited.

Back in London, we stayed with Matt's parents for a couple of days. One evening I walked in on a conversation he was having with his dad, heard him saying ". . . considering how involved I was in the sale, I think I should be entitled to some kind of recognition or commission from Tarisio."

I couldn't help myself.

"Are you talking about my violin?" I said. "I don't understand."

Matt's father came in. "Matt was just saying that he introduced you to Tarisio and found the violin for you. That's right, isn't it?"

He was leading me, just like his son did. I duly followed.

"I suppose he did."

"Well then, it's only right that he should be given credit for that. It's not fair that Matt did all the work to help you find a new violin and Tarisio doesn't reward him. It's just good business."

His tone was pleasant, calm and very sure of his opinion. Good business? Was that what it was? Was I being unreasonable, thinking how wrong this conversation was? Later, alone with Matt, I brought it up again.

"Did you really mean that, that you think you should get a commission for the sale?"

Matt tried to explain. "Not exactly. I definitely don't want a commission from you. But I do want Jason to know that I'm a good salesman. And helped you to make the decision to buy the violin."

I could understand that. That's what he wanted, to be part of the dealing world.

"I know that's your ambition," I said, "but it's very painful for me to have to buy a replacement at all. I wasn't looking to buy a new violin. Doesn't your father realize that? Especially given the circumstances? Do they even know that the violin was with you when it was stolen?"

It was clear they didn't, for later his father chided me gently for leaving the violin "lying around." I couldn't believe it. Again, Matt explained it away by saying, "I thought you didn't want me to talk about it to anyone."

This time I was adamant. "I really want them to know."

"OK. But I need to find the right time."

The right time? For who? "Do it soon," I said. "If you don't, I will."

I was angry.

Maybe he did in time, maybe he didn't. Conversations like that were fuel to the sense that I was living in a different world—one that looked like the old world, sometimes sounded like the old world, but was in fact a sort of demented doppelgänger. It was confusing at the best of times to know where I belonged. And there was Matt, airbrushing out parts of my history, painting other parts in. A little while after the set-to regarding his parents, the subject of the deal, the commission (Tarisio took 20 percent), what was right for him and what was wrong, came up again. He had been quite clever for me. I'd bought the Strad in the States, but not in New York. If you buy an instrument in New York you have to pay a 7.5 percent New York tax, which seems a little steep if you don't live there. Matt had told me about a loophole whereby, if we flew into Newark instead of JFK, there'd be no US state tax to pay. No tax on £250,000. Now he made the suggestion that with the money I had saved I should buy him the bow he wanted for his cello. It never seemed to occur to him that this whole nightmare had been of his making, that I owed him precisely nothing. But that was Matt all over, demanding everything I could give, everything I owned. What was I without him?

Try as he might, he couldn't keep the world at bay forever. I had a violin now. It belonged to me, but it wasn't my violin. But it was a violin. There was a possibility there. I'd paid money for that possibility, understood the nature of the contract. It wasn't like the Bergonzi on the stool, not mine, no use for it. In the back of my mind I could almost picture a use for it.

And now I have to talk about Ian. My *amazing* friend Ian. I've kept away from him for a while, because it's difficult, swamping you with character after character. I've talked about Gerald, now I have to bring in Ian. He won't want me to, but it wouldn't be right, to talk about my life without Ian, because it's Ian essentially who pulled me through this time, kept me sane. So, Ian.

It had been Ian who introduced me to Ricci. I've left him out earlier, there were too many names about, others on the stage, but it's his turn now. Ian turned me around, showed me a different path. He'd done a major tour with Ricci, twenty years ago, just before Ricci retired, thought that Ricci and I could work together, that I needed someone like him. Ian is a pianist but also a conductor, and like a conductor he knows how to bring things together, how this and that might fit. That's what he did for me and Ricci, saw the prospects there, how I could learn, how it might invigorate us both. I'd met him when I was nineteen. He'd invited me to play the Beethoven concerto with him (he conducts the Henley Symphony Orchestra in Oxfordshire) and we'd played together in a concert for Ark, a surgeons' charity. Ian and I really clicked. When I look back on my musical life, the movement of it, I realize how much I learned from Ian. There's nothing in the world I like more than playing with Ian. He's appeared on both my records, playing Beethoven and Brahms. So all this time he was encouraging me to play the repertoire with him; even when I wasn't giving concerts he was still keeping that part of my brain, the performing part, active. It was functioning, not particularly well, but functioning in fits and starts like an out-of-tune motor.

As a pianist (who, as a species, tend not to carry their instrument around from concert to concert), his attitude was quite different from mine. "You're the artist," he'd say, "not the violin," and because he said it in such an encouraging way, with such a sense of goodness and humor and understanding, he kept my feet on the earth and my head above water. He would say, "I understand how difficult this whole thing is. But I want you to remember that it's not the violin that has made you—you can live without it." I didn't quite believe him, but he was persistent, pragmatic. It was so easy for me to think my life was over without the violin. I'd wrapped myself in that armor.

Now, with my new violin, Ian was the one who took the tin opener to that armor, encouraged me to get back on track. "I know you don't want to do solo work but why don't you do something else—chamber?" So I started doing recitals with him. They were very few and far between, but already I could feel the wound beginning to heal. I could touch a violin again, hold one. The pain was slightly lessened.

There was a school friend, a pianist, a sight-reading genius, undisciplined to a degree, with a quickness of mind. Like so many people of turbulent talent, life hadn't been easy for him, and my plight must have touched him. When everything was falling down he got in touch, his ability to read a score traveling way beyond the page. There was a music festival in Yorkshire. He asked me if I'd like to do some playing. Just that: some playing, a nice, bland ask. Go for a walk, have a burger, do some playing. That's what it sounded like, as if it was that easy. I'd never imagined that, it had never seemed possible before, that it could be easy like that, not in the sense that I could or couldn't do it, but that it *didn't really matter*, that nothing depended on it. I said yes, yes I would. It was the height of summer, the countryside at its most soothing best. I loved it. So we just did it for a few months, bits and bobs, here and everywhere. And playing again with somebody who I'd been at school with made me feel as if I was connected to my old life, but in a completely different way. It was as if I was coming back into a world I knew but in a different guise: different approach, different mind and, yes, different violin. My life, my tutors, my parents—they all dropped away.

What is a child prodigy? Here's another stab at it. It's a means to another's end. Oh, they wish you well, wish the very best for you, but there is a price to pay, and the price is you. Now I could play with no expectations, lift a violin with nothing in front of me, precious little behind, just a violin and a cello and a piano, a floor somewhere, a set of chairs, maybe a stage, maybe not, three music stands and the flash of friendship on the others' faces. What's that word I am looking for? Freedom! Free of the past and the present, free of Matt. The concerts weren't advertised. We enjoyed ourselves, the repertoire pleasing, filling in part of the emptiness that lay within me. For the first time in my life, I was playing just for the love of playing. You might think it was about losing myself in the music, but it wasn't quite like that. It was more about finding a new beginning, easy strokes in the shallow end, not treading water, not using a float, but swimming in water that was warm and calm and inviting. No name, just a woman with a violin.

Matt, stranded on the sidelines, didn't like it. He felt excluded, and there is truth in that. He was. It was good to exclude him. I was experiencing an independence I had never felt before. But Matt wouldn't let me be, wanted to be with me all the time—just like at Prussia Cove, only it wasn't funny or endearing anymore. Just wearying, unbelievably wearying. He'd been accepted by a conservatory in Brussels, was due to go in a month or so, wanted me to go with him, expected it. I knew I wouldn't be going, knew that him going to Brussels was the way out for me. There was no way he *wouldn't* go to Brussels. The time that I had wanted for so long, the time I hadn't had the strength or resolve to put into action myself, was moving around the clock. Hours, days, only weeks to go. He was losing control. Perhaps he could sense it too, for there was one time when all his pent-up frustrations came to a head. I was rehearsing with the trio in the chapel where the concert was going to be held and we'd finished early. Matt was wandering about somewhere, I didn't know where. One of the other players said, "Let's go back to our lodge, order a curry, have a bit of a party." I thought, "Great. A curry. A bit of a party." Off we went, had our curry and our bit of a party. A couple of hours later Matt appeared, face like thunder. He'd turned up at the church and found me absent without leave. Back in our room fury, absolute fury, ruled his soul. I fled the room in tears, ran back to the lodge, ended up staying with the other players for the rest of my time there. That was the end. I knew it.

The actual split came two weeks later. Every time I'd brought it up before, he'd fly into a panic, find all the good reasons why it was a bad idea, and we'd fall back into it. Now, though, he had no other strings to pull. He asked me to go to Brussels with him. I refused. It was quite easy to say no, to finally break the tie. I moved back down to London, stayed with Ian for a while, until I found a flat just around the corner from him in Dollis Hill. That was no accident either. I'd had enough of feeling isolated. I needed to be near someone solid and reassuring, someone I could trust and who trusted me. After a few months Matt returned, secured a job at Tarisio. I was glad for him. He'd got what he wanted. He made efforts to keep in touch, but I kept my distance. While we were on speaking terms, there were no friendly get-togethers, drinks or meals. I was done with all that, done with him. I could just enjoy playing again.

That's how it started: some duos with Ian, and the trio, started playing recitals, a little later in music festivals. I just wanted to be with people. It was not so much returning to the stage, but actually returning to the violin. I'd told myself that that part of my life, the solo violinist Min, was over, though what I was to replace it with was very unclear. I'd remembered a story that Ian had told me and it had given me a strange sort of comfort. His mother had been a violinist at the Bournemouth Symphony Orchestra, back in the days when there were very few female violinists. She had four marvelously musical children back at home, and suddenly in the middle of a car park on the way to a concert she'd thought, "I can't do this anymore," and had driven back home. She stopped playing the violin as if it were a full stop at the end of a sentence. Years later, when in her seventies, she'd said to Ian, "It's really strange, but the only people who ever knew I played the violin are you, my children. Nobody else knows I used to play in an orchestra. They all see me as that nice lady who potters around the village." And thinking back on it, in those dark days, I'd thought, "Yes, maybe that'll be me in forty years' time. No one will know at all, perhaps maybe my sister, I'll have vanished, my life as a violinist is over." But with Ian and other friends nudging me forward, it came to me that maybe it wasn't quite over . . . maybe.

A friend of mine's flatmate had started a quartet. He was young, early twenties. It was a talented quartet, but they had a history of falling out with each other. It's not uncommon. The history of quartets is littered with arguments, reconstructions, reunions. The saying about a marriage—that it's only as happy as the unhappiest person—is true of a quartet too. It only takes one unhappy person for the whole thing to fall apart. The ones that last, that know each other inside out, can bring to what they play an almost unfathomable depth. This was not one of those, and their history was almost an attraction. If that's the way it is with them, I thought, then I don't need to commit for very long. They'd lost their first violinist and cellist in a matter of weeks. And they had a tour in Scotland coming up and they didn't have a violinist or a cellist. So my friend's flatmate asked me, "I know you'll probably say no, but we're desperate." I asked what they were playing and he said Schubert and I thought, "Why not? It isn't a life sentence. I could help them with that."

So there were selfish reasons too. Playing in a quartet would help me keep my fingers in shape. The first-violin parts are very demanding; not as deliberately demanding as the solo repertoire, but taxing all the same, and with a different set of demands, different purposes of execution. You're there for a different reason. So I'd be learning too, learning with my new violin, an opportunity for us to get to know each other, discover our strengths and weaknesses, to learn how to play together. But there was another attraction. Chamber music played well is all about connecting with other human beings—you're one of four as opposed to being a soloist. Separate entities but together. And instead of joining a professional quartet I was joining this young group barely out of studenthood. It couldn't have been better, couldn't have meant more. I was fulfilling what I had missed at school and college. Back then, everybody else was forming these little quartets. They never went anywhere, it was something they did purely for fun. I had never been allowed to do that. I'd had my career. Whenever I'd shown any indication to my teacher that I was thinking of joining or forming a quartet, they would always stamp on it firm, insisting, "You're a soloist! Your pedigree is as a soloist! You have to play as a soloist or not at all!" But now, with no pressure to perform, no stage to dominate, I could make my own decisions, forge my own path. Yes, I might be more experienced than anyone else in the quartet but that wasn't the reason for joining. I wanted to taste the kind of student life I'd never had. I couldn't be a proper child again but I could be a sort of student. I could do this *for fun*.

Of course, it became more than that. It was like I was reborn. I was experiencing the world for the second time, but also for the first time. It was so thrilling, living something that I hadn't done before. I was comfortable with the violin again. It was a first for me and my new violin, a new world, a new genre. In the same way as when I'd started with my lost violin, it had been the beginning of my adult career, this young quartet marked the beginning of another life, and we were starting it together. I was able to draw close to it. It made me appreciate its qualities, invited me to explore it, an invitation which for the first time I was ready to accept. Without the quartet, I don't think it would have happened, I wouldn't have been able to bring myself to explore my violin. And because some of those first-violin parts are technically demanding I didn't have time to continue with mourning. I had this one to consider.

There was an odd dynamic going on here too. In one sense I was submerging myself with three others, but at the same time finding a new identity: not Min the prodigy, but Min the player. There was an everyday normality to it that was refreshing, unexpectedly so. On a lot of the programs it still stated the first violinist as the woman who'd left. I didn't even have a name. Who cared who I was? I was part of a quartet. The quartet had a name, and within that name lived the first violinist, alongside the second violinist, the viola player and the cellist. That was enough. That was all anyone needed to know.

We did the Scottish tour. They were doing their masters at Hanover, Germany, and I would fly out with them, play there. We all traveled together, which was, among everything else, the strangest thing of all, the part I found most difficult. I was so used to being on my own, making my own travel arrangements, staying by myself. But if you're in a quartet, togetherness is all. Some nights one of the players even wanted us to eat the same: nothing more, nothing less!

We played a lot of Schubert. I was still feeling broken, glad to be playing again, but with an aching heart, and Schubert seemed to reflect all that lay inside me, all the tears and the sorrow and the memories of happiness. One of the pieces we played most often was *Death and the Maiden*. Schubert wrote it in 1824, shortly after he'd finished another piece for string quartet, *Rosamunde*. The two couldn't be more different, *Rosamunde* full of sweetness and light, *Death and Maiden* with a lyricism tempered by a dark, sometimes furious undertow of desperation and despair. By 1824 Schubert's syphilis had returned. He would have known that the years ahead would be few and, as his illness gathered momentum, debilitating. "Think of a man," he wrote, "whose health can never be restored, and who from sheer despair makes matters worse. Think, I say, of a man whose brightest hopes have come to nothing." Schubert had already written instrumental works based on songs but the inspiration for *Death and the Maiden* was a much grimmer location, where Death confronts a young innocent. "Give me your hand, you lovely, tender creature. I am a friend and come not to punish. Be of good courage. I am not cruel: you shall sleep softly in my arms." It is, of course, reflective of his own life: at one end, Schubert the delightful, romantic creator of song, the toast of Vienna; and at the other, restless, chaotic, solitary, plunging into depths from which he would emerge, but most certainly not unscathed. So here in this piece he touches joy and regret, pleasure and pain. He is alive but touching mortality.

I heard somewhere that the most requested piece of music in hospices is *Death and the Maiden*, and it's easy to understand why. It's a bridge between life and death, and I felt so close to, if not death, then a finality of some sort, that it almost cleansed the darkness within me. It's frightening, but also glorious. He's captured the possibility of another world, and when you're facing the end of yours that's incredibly comforting. "When I attempted to sing of love," he wrote, "it turned to pain. And again, when I tried to sing of sorrow, it turned to love." Nowhere is this more apparent than in this unforgettable, heartbreaking work of art.

Then I had to step away. It was a sad thing to do, but the right one. The other members were approaching their mid- and late twenties, on the brink of emerging into the profession. They needed to enter into the competitive world, and without competitions, winning, getting placed, it's very hard to get noticed. I was nearly thirty-five, and the cut-off point for many of the competitions hovers around that age. So I needed to step back. And the other thing in the back of my mind, talking to me in a small, insistent voice, was that, if I stayed, entered the world of international quartets, it would be a signal that I had abandoned my solo career. I had thought I had. Now, I wasn't so sure. The group had given me so much life, like a blood transfusion. Thanks to them, my heart was pumping some good stuff around me. They had strengthened me, released me from the despair that had held me in thrall for so long. Thanks to them, maybe I would have the nerve to stand on my own two feet again.

And what of the violin? What was happening to my Strad all this time? What sort of bed had it been lying in? Even now, I don't know the whys and wherefores of what went on. The police can't tell me much, stuff they have to keep close to their chests: witnesses interviewed, suspicions roused, money dangled. There are figures out there who need to be kept in the shadows. If their names got out, what they did, they'd be in a whole heap of trouble. So the picture's murky. It's a murky world they're dealing in.

That's not to say the police weren't clear about how to go about it, what their main purpose was: the recovery of the violin. As one of them said later, "This was a violin that has gone through time. It will out-see all of us. We wanted it to go through this time safely." He was right. This would be only part of the violin's story. In a hundred years' time hopefully only a very small part. They're like great trees, these violins, like those from which they're made. They live through epochs.

My violin was born in 1696, the year Peter the Great became tsar of Russia. It's seen off Napoleon, Queen Victoria, Stalin, Mao Tse-tung, two world wars, and, so far, the atomic bomb. People come, people go, violinists live, violinists die, empires rise and fall, and the violin lives on, washed from shore to shore on the tides of wealth, fortune and history. This is but a speck of time for my Strad.

It had been snatched from its current home but it was still a Stradivarius. No one could change the nature of what it was. And it's that which would ensure its preservation. It was worth something, worth a fair amount. And if there's one thing the traveling community know about, it's how to lay things up. Another kind of thief and there would have been worries about how it would be kept, underground perhaps, in the damp, moisture buckling the structure beyond repair, but the folk my violin had landed among knew *exactly* how to do this properly. They've had other stuff in their keeping—guns, jewelery, drugs, all sorts. Looking after valuable things is what they do. And if you have something valuable, you don't throw it away. You keep it as close as you dare. You keep an eye on it.

Mine was not the first famous violin to be stolen, wouldn't be the last. There's a host of them, many which are still out there. The Colossus Strad was taken from Luigi Alberto Bianchi's mother's house on November 3, 1998. The 1727 Davidoff Strad was stolen in 1995 from a locked bedroom closet in Erica Morini's Manhattan apartment. The Le Marien Strad went missing from a shop in Manhattan, the Nicolò Amati disappeared in Tokyo, the King Maximilian Strad in Mexico, and the Mendelssohn, owned by the Mendelssohn brothers—bankers and descendants of Felix Mendelssohn the composer—vanished in Berlin, first stolen by the Nazis, then disappearing from the Deutsche Bank during the 1945 occupation. Most of these thefts were targeted, unlike mine, which for the thieves was probably a pure stroke of luck.

But there would be a price to pay for this luck. And the price to pay is the price of the violin. My violin had value. And that value would never lie still. It would create tensions, sow misunderstandings, arouse deep suspicions. Cracks would appear in the edifice of trust. Old enmities would take root in the fissures, prise trust apart. They'd hitched themselves to this value and, until they were rid of it, they'd have to ride it as best they could. But the value would buckle and twist, upset their equilibrium, throw them off balance. It was difficult to control, impossible to tame. At some point in the future they'd have to try to turn that discomforting ride into as much cash as they could. One day, the violin would have to be brought out into the open, presented for show in a hotel room or a car park—and that is when the new custodians of my violin would be at their most vulnerable. That's how it is with stolen value, it has to be realized, and that was why, as far as the police were concerned, my violin was always, *always*, going to pop up somewhere. It was just a matter of time. But how to play it, how to use their (the police's) intelligence, how to force the thieves' hand—that's the trick.

Andy from the British Transport Police would ring me every Friday afternoon. Often he had nothing in particular to talk about, but there was reassurance in his voice. It meant an awful lot. Later when I asked him why he kept calling, he said it very simply. "When someone dies, the police send family liaison officers who get into that family, who are there for them during the investigation, someone solid for them to lean on. But no one had died in this story and we didn't have a stolen Stradivarius liaison officer, so . . ." Andy recognized that this wasn't something that had simply been stolen. It was part of my life—no, more than that, it *was* my life. I'd bend his ear, go on and on about my feelings. He threw me a rope, pulled me out of the dark waters for a while, gave me a little air to breathe. It's difficult to exaggerate the strength I found through that lifeline. He must have the patience of a saint.

So, to begin with: by the time they have identified the three thieves, the police are a couple of days behind. The news has got out, the nature of the beast they hold, but whether they believe it or not is a different matter. They're a suspicious bunch. It's a tribal thing. They live in an us-and-them world. Outsiders are not to be trusted, particularly outsiders in uniform. What the police might say about the violin will not be believed. It would be seen as a trick to wrong-foot them, to lead them into a trap. But it's vital that they know what it is really worth, the seriousness of the theft, the heat that it is likely to engender. Then they might be able to seek a way forward.

There were two principal figures within the British Transport Police who ran the operation: Andy, and Simon Taylor. Andy ran the day-to-day investigation, Simon was in charge of the covert stuff, the intel. Pretty soon, intelligence came to light that someone might be looking to sell such an item. Approaches were made. The trader was wary, still uncertain what it was they had in their hand. They didn't believe in the world outside—never had. It was a kind of strength for them, though like all strengths, there lay the inherent weakness. They didn't know how to grasp the outside hand. It felt so alien to them. For them to learn of the violin's true value, it had to be done differently. An article in the *Sunday Times* wouldn't help much, nor an announcement in any other paper. They were not the most committed of newspaper readers. It had to be done through a medium in which they would have some faith, in which they would believe, and with which they were completely familiar. Television. They said, "If it appears on the next *Crimewatch*, we'll know it's what you say it is. We'll know there's a deal to be done." They gave forty-eight hours.

For those of you who don't know, *Crimewatch* is the BBC's regular crime-update program. Millions watch it, thieves included. It acts as a sort of noticeboard for them: who's done what, what they have (or haven't) got away with. The police got the theft featured on the show. It was a rush job, but the BBC were terrific. They made room for it. The piece was done as an appeal for witnesses, and though witnesses might help, its primary object was to let the thieves know what they had in their possession. They brought another Stradivarius into the studio. There was an expert who told the viewers how much the violin was worth. Now hopefully the two brothers and their uncle, and all the rest of their two families, would know.

No more trying to sell it to bus conductors in an internet café for under a hundred quid. It was worth a million pounds. What were they going to do about *that*?

The underwriters offered a reward. (From time to time, as the trail ran cold, they'd agree with the police to up the money, create a little stir, wake the value up, jolt the wires a little.) Everyone waited. It was intensely frustrating. They were walking on eggshells. They didn't want to push it but they didn't want to let it slip away. The trouble was, the immediate family they were dealing with weren't very good at this sort of business. A violin worth a million pounds? Way out of their league. The bait had been laid, but no one dared bite. It was too much for them, the landscape too unfamiliar, the risks too great. They didn't have the nous or the confidence. The bait lost its potency. No bite. No sale. The police lined up a priest who had strong links with the community, suggested it could be left in his church. That prayer fell on stony ground.

But there were people within the traveling community who *were* familiar with dealing on this scale, who weren't fazed by what the brothers had lucked onto. Pretty soon they became involved. Ironically, the issue of ownership raised its head. Who did it belong to, the two brothers or their uncle? The police believe that, soon after the theft, a tussle began between the two families, each one staking their claim. One family would come along, take it from one location, move it to another. Then the other family would pitch up and take it back. The violin became a currency in its own right, used as collateral, or to pay off debts. No one played it but its call reached out, compelled them to listen. The Stradivarius magnet.

The three responsible were arrested soon after the theft, before the year was out. It was to be expected. Their faces were well known. The older one (the smallest of the three, who could, one of the police said, "almost fit inside a suitcase") was found at an address north of Ruislip, hiding in a bedroom. The other two boys were swept up swiftly too. One was spotted by the Met, arrested and taken to the police station just off Tottenham Court Road. Within two hours his father rang up, said he was coming in with the lad's brother. It was just before Christmas.

Where was the violin now? They couldn't say. They'd sold it to someone. *Sold it to whom?* They couldn't say. Did they offer it up? Did they ever say, *If we get the violin back, will you drop the charges?* If they did, I never heard of it, and what could the police do? They were always going to be charged. The evidence was too strong. A court might have found the violin's return mitigating circumstances, reduced their sentence, but there was no deal to be had that way.

And by now, the families knew what the violin was worth. What was a clutch of light prison sentences set against a million pounds? Just before the trial came to court, Andy made one of his Friday looking-after-me calls. The matter of the insurance had yet to be cleared up, the violin was long gone, and I was at rock bottom. He could hear it in my voice. He said, "Min, it wasn't your fault. I can hear that you're beating yourself up about this, but as much as I'm a professional and you're a professional, these are professional thieves."

The three went to court. The three were found guilty. The uncle went to jail, the boys given suspended sentences. And I am in a jail, and I am living a suspended sentence and the violin, moving from one location to another, why, that's in a jail too. While I took to my bed, the violin traveled, first around the London area, then farther afield. It's very likely it went up to the big derbies that are held every year—where a lot more than livestock changes hands. Simon Taylor would receive intel from a plethora of places, but nothing 100 percent certain. He didn't want to spook the families, force their hand, make them do something that we would all regret.

So the violin traveled. It used to travel with me, travel with me everywhere, now it traveled with them. What did they keep it in? A sack? A box? A trunk? Was there someone in charge of looking after it, a minder? Was it taken out on special occasions, shown around, a totem to be talked about in a secretive huddle, the passport to a different future? Did they look at it, see it as a thing of beauty? Or was its glow like that of a match lit unwarily in a blackout—a moment of supreme danger, something that should never be done until all the curtains have been drawn? For it would not have lost its glow. Every time the lid was opened, the cloth removed and the body lifted up by the neck, it would have glowed. It can't help itself, its body blushes, its sensuality, its love of the touch. Did they dare to revel in its calm, deafening aura? Did they think about it day after day after day like I did?

On occasion the police would make a move on them, get a search warrant, go in. They were selective with these raids—didn't want to give anyone the impression that they knew more than they *should* know. So they searched the places that were obvious, fair game.

Crimewatch had laid a good base. When the reward was advertised a hotline to the underwriter was set up. Voices called in. Information was graded. But it was a waiting game. The police would lie fallow for a while, then shake the tree, appear suddenly where the boys had lived, carry out another search. About a year down the line, at three o'clock in the morning, they staked out one of the travelers' sites, 99 percent certain that the violin lay hidden in there somewhere. But it was a big site and they couldn't get a warrant to search all of it. They had to walk away. Over the next couple of years there'd be long stretches of suspension, followed by intense moments of activity. There were the sightings. One led them to the Irish Republic, another to Bulgaria. Both false.

(As I write this, news bursts onto the wire—another stolen Strad has been found, this time one that was stolen thirty-five years ago from Roman Totenberg in 1980. The violin, the Ames Stradivarius, was taken from his office in Cambridge,

Massachusetts. Totenberg had worked with Igor Stravinsky, Arthur Rubinstein, Leopold Stokowski and he died in 2012, without ever knowing what had happened to his violin. He suspected he knew who had taken it, but the police didn't feel the suspicion justified a search of the suspect's house. Much later it was revealed that, had they done so, he would have been reunited with it very soon after it vanished. The parallels with my own story are almost too clear to bear. There is a picture of a daughter, looking happy, but how sad it is that Mr. Totenberg was never reunited with the instrument he loved and who loved him, never knew what had happened. Not knowing is one of the very worst things. He'd owned the violin for nearly forty years, and had once spoken about the time it took for him to realize its potential. "It took some time to wake it up," he said, "to work it out, find all the things that it needed, the right kind of strings and so forth." It could have been me speaking.)

Curious as to who else might have suffered the same fate, I Google "stolen violins." On the first site I find the entry is fifty-seven pages long. I scroll down through the list, idly at first, then as the scope blossoms, I read them, gripped, one by one: pictures of violins, cases, bows, a complete, self-contained tragedy in every one. Here's an original Rodolfo Fredi, made in 1922, stolen in Leghorn, Tuscany, on December 19, 2015. Here's a Carlo Fernando Landolfi (1770) made of two first-class quality spruce with even, straight grain, belonging to Nancy Bargerstock, stolen from the back of her BMW, near the Herodes Atticus Theater, in Athens, Greece, on September 5, 1995. The notes, details and photographs are uploaded to the site by the owners, or former owners. Alarnah has CCTV footage of some "creep climbing through my kitchen window on Monday, May 26, 2014" and stealing her French violin, which she thinks bears the label "Jacobus Stainer *in absom prope oenipontum*, 1659." In a remote area, Transkei, in Eastern Cape, South Africa, a small-size violin made by Ifshin Violins of California, a "beautiful reddish coloring [sic] and beautiful sounding instrument" bought for their daughter, was taken from her during a guided trip in November 2013. In the information box, her parents write: "Our daughter is heartbroken for her loss. Need the instrument to use when going back to university. Her scholarships depend on it."

So many people in pain. Heather Barton in Walthamstow says, "It's a Lark violin, worth very little in cash terms, but I loved playing and am upset to lose it." Chattanooga, Barcelona, Brussels, the same story is told over and over again. Does this ring a bell? "My life has been through pain and heartache . . . Everything went downhill . . ." That was Antonio Rivera of Austin, Texas. It could have been me writing. Trains, cars, bus stops, flats . . . it's not a violin that they have lost, it's a part of themselves. Of her 1999 Roman Teller violin, Carrina Smith says, "This instrument has been my voice since I was 14 years old and I am devastated at its loss." The desperation is overwhelming, their cries, their feelings of emptiness echoing my own. "My beautiful violin has been stolen!" "A substantial reward is being offered. No questions asked!"

Suddenly I picture an island of stolen violins in some forgotten ocean, waiting to be rescued, a host of lost violins that have been snatched from their homes, taken from those who loved them. I imagine them gathered on the shore, playing furiously, in the hope that some passing distant ship will hear them, alter its course, rescue them all, restore them into the waiting arms of . . . A violin stolen is an act of cruelty. The violins on these pages are all different. Some are like mine, instruments that possess greatness within their frame, but many do not. But they all speak to those who love them, they all mean so much more than the grain of the wood, the glue and the catgut, the value. All are terrible stories of deprivation. Of her Matteo Goffriller violin, made over three hundred years ago, and lost on January 29, 2008 on the 12:18 train from Paddington to Taunton, Ruth Self writes, "I hope it will be recovered soon and that its beautiful tone can be heard in public again." All loved violins sound beautiful to their owners, just like every baby is beautiful to every mother. It's their own voice they are listening to. Take away the heartache, the anguish, and what's the underlying theme? "I would just like to get it back," says Thomas Gowan, who lost his Stravari student-made violin in Bedford, Ohio, on November 20, 2010. *I would just like to get it back.* Me too.

Finally, the news the police had been waiting for came in. How, I have no idea. All they will say is that work done on the internet led them to a warehouse in the Midlands, where the violin was being stored. It hadn't popped up in a hotel room or a car park, but, nevertheless, had poked its head out into the open air. It was going to be auctioned.

Simon Taylor was in a dilemma. He was fairly certain that this was my violin, but there was no guarantee. Who was offering it up for sale? What about the venue? At the time they weren't even sure about the warehouse's probity (though it transpired that the warehouse was completely above board). It was a tough call. If the police charged in and were wrong, they'd have shown their hand to no effect. They had planned to make their move right after the weekend, but that Friday Simon Taylor had a change of heart. He'd been waiting for news like this for three years. If they left it and went up to the Midlands on Monday only to find it gone again . . . ! As he said, "I just couldn't do it!"

He got hold of Mark at Beare, told him the news. Together they raced up the motorway. Could it really be their Strad? A couple of hours later Simon was knocking on the warehouse door. He'd like to take a look at the violin they had.

"It's a fake," he was told, "a pseudo-Stradivarius."

"I don't think it is," Simon said.

They walked in. Mark took one look at it. He'd carried out repairs on it some years back and recognized his own work instantly—a wonderful moment. I can only imagine it, the beating heart, the dry mouth, your insides flipping over. There it is, lying on a shelf, quiet and patient, waiting for you. My lovely Strad. My lovely, lovely Strad.

5

'M ON A TRAIN. I GET A CALL FROM ANDY, MY ROCK, always calm, always hopeful, always trying to keep me grounded. A sort of angel, ringing in from the land of detection regular as clockwork, always there to look out for me. But there's something different in his voice, I can tell, I can tell.

"We've got it! We've found it!"

I could hear it in his voice. Pleasure for me, and a vindication of the police's many years of hard, patient work. They'd had faith in the violin, faith in its ability to survive, the same as me. They didn't love the violin like I did, had never met it, but had formed an almost personal connection to it. They've found it! They've got it!

A world of emotions sweeps through me, relief, elation, a longing to reach out, embrace it to have it in my arms again, to lavish it with caresses and kisses, to do all that, to hug it tight (can that be right?), physical, physical, physical, but at the back of it, or in the pit of all these feelings, a gnawing realization that things are not the same as they were. Times have changed. I have changed. Maybe the violin has too. Has it? Does it still possess the sweet voice that lay within it? And can this Min, such a different Min than it was used to, persuade it to sing again? Or is it wounded, damaged, crippled? Have things been done to it?

And there's that other obstacle. I can't speak it yet, but I know it, have known it ever since I took the check. The violin no longer belongs to me. It belongs to the insurance company. I took their money. I paid off debts. I bought another violin. I funded my reconstructed life and now . . . oh my goodness. They've found it! And yes, it's all in one piece, in the case that Ricci gave me, with the two bows and even the sheets of music that were there when it was taken.

I quickly lost count of all the dealers who called me, congratulated me, passed on their good wishes. The world of the solo artist was inviting me back into the game again. My violin was found. It would only be a matter of time until . . . I gave a media interview the afternoon after the violin was recovered, the only one I did, and for the British Transport Police. They'd been so good to me, it was the least I could do. It was a happy story for them. The good guys had won. The girl got her violin back. They deserved it. It was late August. Ian said I could give the interview in his garden. Even that was hard, because even then I wasn't sure how it would turn out.

It was back, but the likelihood of being able to keep my violin was slim. (Let me say that again, to relive the strangeness of it: the likelihood of being able to keep *my* violin was slim.) The insurance company had called me that same day, very soon after Andy phoned, straight as a die. As per my agreement with them, I was given first option, ninety days to decide what I was going to do. All I had to do was pay back the money they'd paid out, and the violin would be mine again. Three months to get my act together. But I didn't have the money, wasn't as strong as I used to be. (I used to be strong! I used to be a performer. I had to be strong!) The will, the means to fight, had been sapped right out of me, but I still retained a glimmer of hope, a weak light in a dark room, about to flicker out. I spoke a lot. I said nothing. In the garden the last rose of summer was drooping and fading. I clung to that.

I asked the insurance company whether I could see my violin, but I wasn't allowed to, not until I'd paid out and not until they were ready to hand it over. Although it was still in one piece, Mark, the luthier at Beare, who had gone with Simon to identify it and had accompanied it back to Beare's vaults, had examined it and thought there might be a crack in it. Might be. It was hard to tell. So before anybody did anything, the insurance company wanted the violin repaired. They wanted to hand it back to me in the same condition as when it was taken. It was a perfectly reasonable stance and quite typical of them. They're very understanding about the lifestyle of a musician, tailor their policies to the needs of a player and work closely with Beare. Though the value of an instrument may run into millions, they understand that, as a player, you're not going to put your instrument in jeopardy and so offer by far the best (and affordable) policies for instrument holders. So they've always been very helpful, and this time was no exception.

Ninety days. It seemed like a long time, but it wasn't really. I tried to get a loan, but I needed over half a million pounds, and nobody would come through. I barely had an income. I reached out to Beare, but Beare was going through its own problems at the time. Other dealers were equally unhelpful. Remember, I'd bought another violin, and a replacement bow. Perhaps I could raise some money on them. I wouldn't be asking for anything more than I'd paid. No chance. The only way I could get money from them was if

I put them on consignment, which meant the dealers would only pay me once they had sold them. That was no use. There was no guarantee that they'd be sold within the ninety days. What's more, the dealers would still want their 20 percent commission, which would mean I'd need to sell the violins, the bow, for more than they were worth. The idea of finding another buyer who'd be willing to pay that sort of money in that time frame was out of the window. So no joy there. The banks wouldn't lend me any money—all they can think of is numbers, and I didn't have any. My bank manager was terribly apologetic, but what could she do? Her hands were tied. Phone calls, waiting for responses, setting up meetings, ringing around, talking to companies, it all took time. I got turned down by everybody. Who was I? What record did I have? Where was the string of forthcoming performance bookings?

What had I got to show for my life? It was gone, and had been gone for two and a half years. Meetings were mirages of hope, fading into nothing when decision time came; no one was interested. And the more you're turned down, the more you start to panic. You start to think you're unclean, untouchable, that there's a mark on your head, or a placard around your neck, failure in your eyes and the way you stand. Nowadays, there are schemes, ways that enable players to join a consortium of investors, but they weren't so prevalent then. I'd never even heard of one, didn't even think of it as a possibility. I'd never been in that situation before. The violin was there, reaching out to me, but as the days rolled by the possibility of us being reunited grew more and more unlikely. I could almost feel it drawing away, shrinking from my grasp. I was losing it again!

Matt calls. Yes, I know, I'm slipping in and out of tense here, but such things, the tremors they have caused, are so vibrant it's like music, the words springing out alive. So, Matt calls. And I'm happy to take his call, glad that he's rung, because he's the person who actually lived it with me. It's easier for me to talk to him about it all than almost anyone.

We agree to meet, not just to meet, but do that other thing I'd always dreamt of doing. Celebrate its return. So we meet in Marylebone, in a bar just around the corner from Tarisio's London office, where he now works. We have champagne. We raise our glasses. The violin's back! I don't know what's going to happen, but the violin's back! It's a miracle in a way. People had always warned me not to get my hopes up, that it was most likely gone forever, but hope was only the half of it. I *knew* it would return. Throughout that time I was still connected to it, and I know now too, as I write this, that I always will be. The "goneness" of it was mine and my violin's, no one else's. Through all that time, the violin was reaching to me and I to it, calls in the air, strands in the ether. I can hear you! Its voice resonated within me, and mine in it. As Andy had always said, it was just a matter of time. It just felt so right that it was still in one piece, another moment of salvation across the march of centuries. I felt alive, extraordinarily alive. Maybe I could be in one piece again too. Maybe we could be one piece together.

And then Matt asked the inevitable question. "What next?"

I give the inevitable answer. "I don't know."

I told Matt that they wouldn't show me the violin until Mark had repaired the damage. Matt starts quizzing me about what I'm going to do. Of course, he knows everything.

He says, "How are you going to raise the money before the deadline?"

"I don't know. I could start with the Strad I bought from Tarisio. Remember, I bought it with the explicit understanding that I could return it immediately if my violin was ever found . . ."

"But what about the rest? You've given your parents a significant sum, paid off other debts plus you don't have the same guarantee with other dealers for the bows you've bought. You'll have to put those on consignment."

"I know. Although Florian [another dealer] has indicated that if it's to help me buy my violin back, he'll make an exception."

"What about the bow from Isaac? I'm guessing he won't buy it back from you, right?"

"I've spoken to his partner. Unfortunately not."

"So even if we gave you back the money you paid for the violin, you'd still be a few hundred thousand short?" We? I noticed it right away. So this was an official meeting?

"Yes," I said. "Still be short."

"And you can't get a loan in such a short time."

"I've tried but the maximum I can borrow is not nearly enough."

"Well, the only way, then, is your parents' house."

"Well, obviously I'm not going to force them to sell their home."

"No, of course not."

Silence.

"Let me talk to Jason. I'm sure he'll be happy to help."

I say, "What does that mean?"

He says, "Let me just talk to Jason and see what he can do."

Well, that sounded fantastic. I didn't know what it meant, but it sounded fantastic.

I met him at Tarisio's. Jason told me that Matt had explained the financial situation to him. He offered to loan me what I needed as a bridging loan, but at an interest rate of 20 percent. I thought, Gosh, that was quite a considerable take! I couldn't even consider it; 20 percent was just too much.

And the ninety days were clicking on by, day after day. I was running out of time. I was feeling really despondent, ready to walk away. Mark from Beare rang me, and said, "I think we have to take the top off." I was nervous about that. Taking the top off a violin is a major operation. It's like open-heart surgery, not to be taken lightly. A lot of things can happen when the top is taken off. Put it back on again, and you can be closing the lid on a completely different violin. Something's happened, something's changed, something's gone that you can't get back. There's always the risk that it may cause more damage than is already there. But Mark was the expert. He knew what he was talking about.

I began getting texts from Matt. Tarisio didn't like the idea at all. "Are they definitely taking the violin apart? Jason thinks it's irresponsible and unnecessary." Am I allowed to see it? No I am not. "Can't you exercise your option *before* surgery? Jason would be happy to talk if you wanted." I was in two minds myself. I asked around my trusted luthiers. They all had different opinions. It didn't matter. Beare exercised their right as the custodian of the instrument. They took the top off. And they were right to do it. They found a touch of damage, not life-threatening, but something that needed to be fixed—a small crack on the left side of the belly. They reinforced the structure with tiny wooden studs. Now the violin and I were almost ready to meet. There was just the small question of the cash.

I had another meeting with Jason. This time I asked Ian if he wouldn't mind coming to the meeting. I needed someone to help me through the maze of options. Jason said he'd thought about it. Clearly I couldn't buy this violin back. It was really sad but that was the reality. I couldn't afford it. But, he said, "I'll help you. Tarisio will loan you the bulk of the money, £400,000, interest-free," and he would find "an anonymous donor" to come up with the rest, at an interest rate of 20 percent, if I let Tarisio sell the violin after I got it back. Tarisio wanted the commission, but they also wanted the publicity. It was a great story and they'd be at the center of it. Figures were coming at me fast. But it was clear what it all boiled down to. I couldn't keep my violin. Tarisio would buy it back for me, then sell it on for whatever they could get. True, I'd get a percentage of the sale, so I wouldn't lose out altogether, but . . .

Goneness was staring me in the face again. I tried to hold on to a semblance of dignity, for the violin as much as myself. I said that I could see that I'd have to sell it, but that I didn't want it to go to auction. There were a number of reasons. The first was personal. In an auction you have no idea who the violin is going to end up with, whereas in a private sale you retain some control. I wanted it to go to a proper player, a professional, someone who would know how to play it, who could realize its potential, fulfill its destiny. Players come, players go; not everyone would find it right for them. That's why, in private sales, the potential buyer is allowed to keep the instrument for weeks at a time—sometimes months—to allow them enough time to get to know the instrument before making a decision. It's a crucial part of the courtship, and says as much about the relationship you form with your dealer as with the instrument itself.

Great dealers are matchmakers, always looking to find the one instrument that will suit you, that could become your perfect partner—for life. Years ago, long before the Strad, I fell out temporarily with one who showed me this Camilli. I tried it out for a couple of weeks, almost bought it. But then, I thought, It's just not really my violin, told him so. He got annoyed and I got annoyed and we parted not on the best of terms. Years later I bumped into him, both of us older and wiser, and we started over again, and he's been really good to me. While all this was going on, I'd keep running into him. There I'd be, the story of my woes on the tip of my tongue. But I didn't tell him. Min didn't do Stories of Woe. She was still under the yoke of Best Face Forward. And later, when I found a voice of my own and told him what had happened, he'd said, "If only I'd known. It would have been so easy to get together investors for you. It's not like you're starting your career." Too late. Too late.

It was important to me to ensure that my violin had an owner who would be a match for it. I owed it that much. A keen and wealthy amateur was not what my violin deserved. They could never bring it to life. They wouldn't have the skill or the time. Simple as that. It would be a waste, and it had suffered too many recent years of neglect for that. It isn't a country-house/drawing-room violin. It's an Albert Hall/Carnegie Hall violin.

The second reason I didn't want it to go to auction was financial. It's well known that auctions rarely fetch the best prices. Most auctions are markets where dealers can buy instruments at more or less wholesale prices. It's something of a cattle market. There are usually only one or two days when the instruments are on show. If you're lucky, you might get an hour or so to try out the one you're interested in. The risk of buying something that might be wrong for you is quite high. There's also the question of provenance. If you buy through a dealer, you get a guarantee of purchase. If something they say is genuine turns out not to be, there is redress. That's not the case in an auction. There, the onus is placed on the buyer to ensure they know what they are buying. The risk is greater, the sums involved more cautious.

At this point, Ian stepped in. He didn't like the set-up, sat me down, told me I had to think this through properly, with a cool head. If I couldn't buy it back, all that was going to happen was that the insurance company would sell it on to someone like Tarisio's and they'd make all the profit on a violin that rightfully belonged to me. He said, "*I'll* lend you what you need so you don't have to pay *any* interest to Tarisio's anonymous donor." He was doing his best. The money I'd make from the sale would help a little. Even if I never played professionally again, still a possibility—no, more than that—a racing certainty, the direction I was heading in. I thought I'd come through the bad times. I thought the trios, the quartets, had cured me of all that, but look what was beckoning me now. A violin not gone but wrenched out of my hands, alive and well and out of my hands. Soon I'd never see it again, never hold it, never hear us sing. It was still gone, and so was I. Trios, quartets, were chimera. Back to bed, turning off that phone, seeing that nothing again, that big warm nothing rolling over me.

Jason was adamant that I shouldn't talk to any of the other dealers. He was concerned that if Beare got wind of our agreement they would somehow manage to tighten their grip on my violin. He wanted me to be positive, had my best interests at heart. I'd bought my current violin from him; he wanted me to remember how happy I was with it. Maybe he believed that. Let's say he did. I drank it in. It was like a drug. It kept me in a kind of fug. What Jason was saying started to sound right. My Strad was not doing me any good at all. Something in the back of my mind started to reject it. I was easy to convince. I didn't question him, because it was too difficult even to get out of bed. He was the professional in the world that had abandoned me, and Matt was our go-between. Matt and Jason. Jason and Matt. They took complete control over my emails, rewrote those that I wrote to luthiers and dealers. I was relieved to comply. Now that any idea of getting the violin back was impossible, in my strange way I was attempting to cling on to some kind of warped professionalism, to go blindly along with those in the know, those who still belonged to that world. Everything was fuzzy like a long-distance telephone call, the voices I was hearing from another land, another time.

And that's what we agreed to. Ian raided his investments and savings and lent me the bulk of my share of the money. Tarisio loaned me the rest. The money was wired in, and I wired the money out. For a short time, on paper, the violin would technically belong to me. On paper it would belong to me. To me. A couple of times I rang Jason and said, "What if I don't want to sell it?" That got a tough legal response. A contract was a contract. I'd have lawyers thrown at me, no doubt about it. And if I pulled out of the sale I'd still owe them for the commission.

I look back on what I have written here. If it makes out that Tarisio are bad, malign, it's come out a bit wrong. I was unsettled when I started writing this book; I'm a little less unsettled now. Tarisio, Jason, Matt: they're dealers. They live in a dealer's world. They have their own priorities, their own way of looking at things. They were right. I couldn't raise the money. I did have another violin. I had no God-given right to the Strad. As Ian had pointed out to me, it didn't belong to me anymore. Not my fault, but not Tarisio's either. But what Tarisio never understood, even in the vaguest of ways, was the fact that, without the theft, my violin would never have left me, not until I was dead. Those ten years I'd spent everything I had on that violin. I'd lived in a shoebox because of that violin, all the money I earned had gone to its upkeep, its refinement. Never on me. Always, the violin came first. That's the difference between a violinist and a dealer. For the dealer the violin is business: good business, bad business, brilliant business. They have offices and catalogs, auctions and showrooms, they fly the world with their violins and cellos and violas, row upon row of them; they buy, they sell, they *deal*. That's not the player's world. The player has their violin and that's it. There is nothing more. Nothing else counts.

What upsets me now is not Matt or Jason, what upsets me is how I let it get like that. It isn't even quite anger, it's more like a kind of wonder. How did I end up being maneuvered in such a way? What made me sign a contract I didn't need to, that bound me in Tarisio's chains every step of the way? Who was I listening to? Certainly not my own voice.

But whose? I could portray Tarisio as an organization tower-
ing over me, wheedling their way into my resolve, but what
were they doing wrong? They saw an opportunity, a woman
rendered helpless, unable to stand up, to go out and fix this,
to take control. Why wouldn't they do what they did? In a
way, they were right. They *were* doing it for my benefit. Was
I showing any signs of resolve? What made me so . . . *incapable*? I still don't understand it, how I let myself be talked into
it all. I still hadn't learned that it's OK to say no. I was in my
thirties and still saying yes, still concerned about not putting
people out, being true to my word. I'd said yes. It was what
I'd always said: yes to being told *how* I should play, yes to
what I should play, yes to Grigori, yes to Ricci, yes to Mother,
to Father, to Matt.

Yes, yes, yes, all my life. Had I ever said, "Actually, I've
changed my mind? I'm thinking, 'No!'" Impossible. I was
brought up to obey. The only freedom I found was the freedom in performance, the only time I was myself. I knew that
much by now, but it didn't help when I wasn't performing.
At all other times I was positioned, maneuvered, moved from
one place to another, one state to another, picked up, put
down.

Two days later, after the cash had been cleared, I was allowed to see my violin. It was still at Beare. I wanted to see
it and yet I was in such a mixed bag of emotions, reality and
wishfulness swirling in my head, that I asked a friend to
come along with me for support. The idea of the world pitted
against me and the violin was just too much. He wouldn't do
anything, he'd just be there.

At Beare, Steven had an assistant there poised with a video
camera. "It would be great for your PR," he said. It was a big

thing for them too, the girl with the stolen violin—a story of redemption, and Beare in the middle of it. Only they weren't anymore. They'd been frozen out and I'd promised not to say anything. I am sure Steven must have sensed the strangeness of my mood. I should have been crazed with happiness, and there I was, looking as if I was attending my own funeral. I said no, no publicity. I just couldn't take it. Steven was puzzled, asked me what I was going to do, now that I had two violins. All I could say was that I had some difficult decisions to make, and left it at that, the words numb in my mouth.

I stepped out onto the street. Tarisio's was a couple of streets away. I was carrying the violin in my hands, the violin and the case and everything in my life lying within the clasps. I was on a London street carrying my past, but not, it seemed, my future.

It was mid-October, the light dull, the sky cloudy, rain starting to spit. The air was chilly, unsettled, and I was carrying turmoil in my hands. Flights of marvelous fancy came to me. What if I kept on walking? What if I didn't turn the corner, cross the street, walk up the Tarisio steps? (Jason had been calling me all morning, asking if I'd got it yet, keeping tabs on me. Maybe such sudden thoughts had been going through his head too.) I was holding my violin and, if I kept on holding it, never let it go, I could step outside the law. I could keep on walking, catch a bus, go to the flat, fish out the passport and fly to Cuba or Venezuela, give concerts in Havana or Caracas, the violin and me, happy in the shade of the tropical sun. The girl with the fugitive violin. My heart pounded with possibilities, but the possibilities weren't possible. I was a professional. I did as I was told. I'd have been laughing if it hadn't been so grotesque.

I got to Tarisio, the mood there excited, buoyant, almost carnal. They couldn't wait to get their hands on it. They've moved since, but they lived in a pretty impressive place even then, more or less an entire building, Jason and his wife in an apartment on the top floor, a rather grand showroom on the first, offices at the back.

They're waiting for me, not at the main entrance, but up on the first floor. I walk up the stairs. They buzz me in, Jason, Matt, a couple of girls who work there. They're all smiles (why wouldn't they be?). I am the girl with the violin, standing there. The men in front of me, who will take it from me, are waiting, not like vultures exactly, but as if they are doing me a favor, all grace and generosity.

This is how it has to be, Min. This is the way of the world. It was your violin. Now it's ours. Once upon a time I lived in a fairy-tale world. Once upon a time I was a young girl who loved playing. Once upon a time I was a young woman who had found her soulmate, who had loved and cherished it as only a young woman can, with the total simplicity of her soul. Once upon a time she and her violin walked in light. Once upon a time . . .

We walk past the open office into the showroom—a nearly rectangular room, a table up in between the two large windows, looking down over Queen Anne Street, red Victorian buildings on the other side. It's a high-ceilinged room, bare, light-colored walls, a sofa at one end, a fireplace at the other. It's trying to feel like a drawing room, but doesn't quite succeed. It's a business venue, everything designed to clinch the deal. A cello sits on display in a holder next to the mantelpiece. I place the case on the table, the old case that Ricci gave me. Now, I am pleased to see it. The funeral threads are dropping off. It's lovely to see this tatty old friend again. "Your violin case is too heavy!" Ricci had said to me. "Here, take this one!" And I'd taken it and placed my violin within it, never thinking that we would ever part. Now it lies on the table, and inside lies my violin. They were never parted. That was good.

I ask if I can spend some time with it. I think if I hadn't asked I wouldn't have been given that time. It would have been an admission on their part, of who it truly belonged to, of what had happened to it, an admission of failure, or if not failure then desire, possession, the way of the world. They agree. They troop out of the room.

෴

I open the lid.

It's almost as I left it: my two bows, the music for the Schubert trio. Only my silk scarf is missing, the scarf I used to wrap it up in. I look down upon it. It looks so familiar, so very much part of me. It's almost impossible to believe that it ever went away. It has a mark, a tiny indentation, on the right-hand side, quite high up, that has gone black over the years. It looks like a teardrop, a tiny show of vulnerability, a plea almost for kindness and love.

"Hello," I say.

I lift the violin up. The room falls away. My friend is there but I am alone now. I notice right away that the bridge is different. It still has the same strings (amazing!) but the bridge that carries them is new. I did a lot of work on the bridge, lowered it, repositioned it, now there is another one in its place, beautifully reconstructed, a work of real craft, but not the old bridge, the bridge we worked so hard on, the bridge that came just right for the two of us. So, my violin hasn't come out of this unscathed either.

I put the violin to my chin. It is like I rediscovered my arm. Does it nestle in, wriggle a bit with the familiar comfort of it all? It sure feels like that, sure feels like *it's back*. It's hard to put on paper. I was talking to Charles Beare the other day about it, how you explain the relationship between a player and their instrument. It's difficult to comprehend. It can't be maternal quite, or paternal, yet it's melted your body. It isn't like a false leg, and it isn't like a baby. People who don't quite get it compare a violin to a child. I can see the reason: the size, the posture, the care you take of it. I've done it myself in this book. It's a useful shorthand, an understandable approximation. But it isn't quite like that. It's something else. It's an expression, that constant unknown inside you, the unspoken being that we all have deep inside us, that's you and you alone. You can't put it precisely into words, or paint it, or sing of it, but you can try, in the hope that one day you might reach out and . . . But you never will. You know you won't. No one ever has. It's the thing which remains always out of reach. We live and we die and we never know quite what it is.

So I hold it to my body, my arm as it should be, my fingers around the neck, everything just so. I play a few open strings, G, D, A, because that's what I always do: G, D, A. I try the E string. It sounds like a bell ringing out from some old and glorious tower, a witness to time. Vibrations run down my arm, into the rest of me, into the room, my head and my lungs and the very core of me pulsating again. Life! I have life in my blood. I've had the Sleeping Beauty kiss. I'm awake again, the spirit of the violin merging with mine. And those three years? They're gone.

Someone asked me later whether it felt as if the violin hadn't been played for some time, whether I was aware of having awakened the violin, in the same way the violin had awoken me, and to be honest, I didn't think about that at the time, didn't want to think of the neglect or the harm or the danger it had been through. It was in my arms again and that was all that mattered. It had been damaged, had a crack that wasn't there before, but that only added to its susceptibility to fortune, to its need for guardianship, understanding, love. And here we were, both of us wide open to each other again. That's what giving your life to art is, a surrender of your life.

I play those open strings again and again, listening to its new vulnerability, finding ways past it. The room is filling now, filling with the violin's energy, my energy. Of course I have awoken it! Of course, but I don't say it or think it. I play it. I play it as I have always played it. As I always knew I could.

I start playing the slow movement of the Brahms. There was really nothing else I could play. I was starting up again from where we had left off. I imagine, had I kept it, this is what I would have returned to. I start with the little passage that's not exactly an arpeggio but a run into the main theme. I know what I am doing. I am saying goodbye to the violin, but captured too by the beauty of the piece, the clarinets and the violin, all in magical, perfect fourths. I had been a custodian of the violin and now it was leaving me, to go into other (unknown) hands. Whose I did not know. Would they have the skill, the attention? What would be their purpose, owning my violin? I did not know, yet I was holding it and comforting it and trying to give it all I could one more time. The violin kept on going higher and higher. You think that it can't go any higher, that it's impossible, what Brahms is asking you and it to do, but you do it, reaching higher still. It's as if it's leaving this world, beyond our cares and misfortunes.

Now I shed it all, not just the room but time itself. This is the violin and only the violin. The violin is timeless, the music too. Only I am temporal, and I have almost disappeared. I am saying goodbye but a goodbye that is physical, a last pouring of myself into the violin—the strings and the wood and the glue, all of it—my life, my troubles, our moments of glory, all of that too. I am merging with it, absolute, playing in full flow, holding nothing back, nothing outside of us, nothing in between. We climb up those notes, higher and higher. It's like going beyond the earthly world.

We reach the top, suspended, all we have known, have lived through, shimmering within us. What is it, passion, death, that spark of beyond? Is this the moment I have lived for? If only I could hold it, if only there were no need for anything else . . . if only life were . . . Then the cascade comes, down we go, into the depths of delicious acceptance, the sad and the wonderful and the bittersweet. It's coming to an end. Not yet, please, not yet, there's still . . .

The door flings open. Matt walks in, beaming. And I am . . . What? I stop, blinking. It's like a bedcover flung back, an intimacy intruded upon.

"How are you getting on?" he says.

How am I getting on? *How am I getting on?*

Did I hand it back? Did he move toward me? I gave it back to him, I am sure of it, but can't remember how. I would have been holding it and he would have moved toward me, believing, what, that the way I was holding it was an invitation for him to . . . reclaim it? Yes, I was holding it, and yes, somehow it was taken from me again, not slid out from under a table by strangers and run out the back door with, but taken away calmly in broad daylight, in a pretend drawing room, with smiles from the man my violin and I had once trusted.

I went home. It felt as if the air had been sucked out of me, my spirit on the floor again. The room was big and there was sky outside. Surely there was room in the world for us, and I could leave, with the sun in the heavens and the violin under my arm—leave to the future what had always been mine, ever since I'd bought it. I'd almost been fooled that I'd got it back, that everything was all right, that it lay there against me, the music flowing out of us forever and ever. And now . . . I was shutting down again. I could feel it, draining out of me, limbs heavy, brain like a wet sponge, chest tight, the great nothing rolling toward me, wave after wave after wave.

History was repeating itself. I hadn't recovered at all. The violin was still lost, could still be missing, as far as I was concerned. I had let it go again, not at the Pret in Euston station but as good as. A gathering of men had come and whisked the violin away from me, men whom I knew, men whom I'd trusted, the tools of their trade words of reason and cajolement. The only difference between them and the thieves was that now, it looked like I'd *never* get my violin back.

I spent about three months in a daze, couldn't get out of bed, couldn't talk to the media, struggled to function. Here we go again.

In the daze I skyped Jason, who was over in New York, and said, "I don't want to sell." I knew it was a useless thing to say, and he knew it too. "Don't worry," I said. "I know I have to sell it. I'm just sharing with you that I don't want to. I really don't want to." It was a last goodbye, a cry into the wilderness. I really didn't want this wilderness. There was an oasis out there, but for me, it was a mirage.

Now Tarisio changed their mind. Waiting for a private sale, they said, was a bad idea. It needed to go to auction. It had to be a positive thing, didn't I see that? Dragging it out would do me no good at all. I had a new violin now. It was time I moved on. It was like the death of a partner. I agreed with Jason that he would sell it in their 2014 auction. Fine. A few weeks later he phoned, saying he wanted to bring it forward to 2013 and create a special auction for its sale. He was losing money. I could see his point, though of course there was another reason, which didn't strike me then. Six months and I might have woken up, come to my senses, found some backers with money. The contract ensured he wouldn't lose out but still . . . if I'd been fired up enough, strong enough.

The sale was a shambles. Although the auction took place on December 18 (four years after it had been taken from me), the bidding had gone live in November. Within minutes, Tarisio had a bid in. Jason called me a little later to say it was the fastest bid they'd ever had. He was pleased, excited. "We've had a lot of interest. You should be very happy." I was taken aback. I could see that, for Tarisio, money was the objective. But for me? I had secretly been fantasizing that no one else would want my violin, that somehow it would find its way back to me. Had Jason forgotten that I was in love with my violin, that I had never wanted to let it go? Now I knew. It had gone from me, maybe forever.

As promised, they'd made a big thing of it, the special

occasion, with new glossy photos and publicity in the national newspapers. It was good for Tarisio, but not for my peace of mind. Come the day, the hour, I was on my way with Ian to a concert. I didn't want any part of it—but that didn't stop me wanting to know. It was like a beloved forced to marry someone else, the last thing you want to hear, but your ears burn for the dread news. Those first few hours, phone and internet lines open, they had nothing, no calls, no takers, no frantic bidding. Not what they had expected or indeed hoped for. Then ten minutes before it was due to close, a second bid came in. There's a rule that if a bid comes in at such a late stage they hold the auction open for another ten minutes, which is indeed what they did. And in that ten minutes came the final bid that would buy my violin. It was done. It belonged to someone else now. It was over. My violin and me, it was over.

The hurt didn't stop right there. The buyer took until the very last day in May to pay. All that time Ian was suffering. He'd emptied his savings to help me out. Every time the buyer missed a payment deadline—and he missed two of them—he was losing out (and Jason too). Meanwhile my violin was locked away in Tarisio's vault, lying in the dark. I found myself asking, "What are my rights here? Tarisio doesn't own it, but neither does the outfit who've bought it. Why can't I play on it at least?" But that was a can of possibilities that would never get opened; too much at stake, too much volatility. Who's to say what I would do if I had it in my possession again for any real length of time? So the idea of playing, playing anything, became a forbidden territory again. The Castelbarco wasn't working either. Every time I picked it up, it felt dead in my hands. It knew me well enough by now, knew I wasn't up to playing it, could do nothing with it, so it didn't try either. So I stopped playing. After the quartet and the trio, the warm waters of friendship and encouragement, all went cold and chilly. I was finding it hard to breathe, no air, no oxygen.

"WHAT'S IT LIKE TO BE A CHILD PRODIGY?"

REPRISE

I had a showdown with my parents. The violin, what had happened, opened up so many things about me, and who I was, who I had been—the child prodigy. And I ended up screaming at my mother, my dear mother, who has always, *always* done her best for me, that she didn't understand, that I'd given my life for her and everybody else and it had all come to NOTHING! GONE! Out it came, all the bile within me, all the childish hurts and some adult ones too.

My mother had a vision of me, they all had, and I would feel a tremendous sense of rejection if I didn't fit into that picture. I wasn't a million miles from the Min she wanted me to be, but I was a human too, not a Min, but a human. I was meant to be perfect. And how does a small girl who's growing remain perfect? How does she try to keep hold of the thing that defines her, that no one, *no one*, wants to go away—same look, same voice, same obedience, *same size*? She doesn't eat. And it came back to me, the burden I'd carried, the light, impossible burden I'd carried for five long and lonely years, the part of being a child prodigy that was hidden away, the dieting elephant in the room. Back in the good old days, the Purcell School years, I didn't eat.

I had anorexia, and everyone, but *everyone*, whether they knew it or not, was on anorexia's side, not mine.

The reason? If only I knew. One, we weren't a demonstrative family. It wasn't Korean to show your feelings with hugs or kisses. When my mother wanted to show affection, it would come via the kitchen and the stove and on to the plate—it would come in the form of food. She'd make my favorite food, lay it down on the table, watch me eat it. Nothing much would be said, it was all in the preparation and the cooking and the eating of it. But now the whole house was in disarray. My father had come back, didn't know how to be a father any longer. He had two growing daughters to contend with. We didn't want to listen to him, and he couldn't hear us anyway. The whole family was foundering. Our parents were caught up still trying to maintain this crumbling edifice of Korean discipline, while Western life was raging outside, changing us (and, did they but know it then, them). But it wasn't all them. There was the matter of who I was too, or rather who I was *going* to be. Yes, that was it. Who was I going to be?

I can pinpoint when it started, the trigger for it, almost to the minute. I was eleven, starting to grow, aware of the changes. I was with a girl about six years older than me, tiny, very, very beautiful, Korean. She had the aura of how I imagined a princess might appear, poised and perfect, born to the red carpet of life. I was idly eating a bowl of pasta, and halfway through she said, "Are you really going to finish that?" I looked up, a little surprised by the question, said that I was. And she replied, "Aren't you worried about getting fat?" "No," I said, "I haven't thought about it." And I hadn't. Until that moment I truly hadn't. And then it came, the knockout blow. Let's put it down in a single line.

"Nobody wants to see a fat performer."

A fat performer. Was that what I was going to be if I didn't watch out? It stuck in my head, went round and round, the fat performer newly in my sights. It was just before my competition in Italy and, from that moment on, I became very mindful not to eat too much, to lose weight. And guess what? I started to feel great. I felt lighter, more energetic. I liked the idea of being in control of what I put in my body—I wasn't in control of much else. I liked being lighter, more energetic. That was the way I should aim to be, less weight all around, in my head and on my bones. And if that hadn't been enough, back at the college, one of the pianists there sang out, apropos of nothing, "You're a lot fatter than your sister, aren't you?"

That was it. That's when it started. I didn't need love and I didn't need food. I had the violin. Wasn't that enough? Eleven, twelve, I managed it. But it didn't get serious, didn't kick in to its full capacity until two years later, after the trouble with Felix in Gstaad. My body had taken a knock, my trust too. No one had looked after me there. No one, apart from the foreign doctors. After that I decided that I would eat only every other day. I made a diary of what my weekly intake was going to be.

So I had problems. Who could I turn to? The school knew, could see that something wasn't right. They weren't the only ones. "Don't let people know you're ill," a piano tutor said to me. "It will kill your career." The school did send my mother a letter, asked her to keep an eye on me, but her reaction was much the same, only more intense.

She was upset, like them worried that if it came out managers and agents wouldn't touch me, angry with me that it had got this far, was out in the open for everyone to see. "But Mum," I said, "I need to go to see someone, a doctor." She was scared and out of her depth. Anorexia simply didn't exist in her world. Growing up as a war child, when food was scarce, and her brother had to catch rats and fish for survival, she would berate me for inflicting this on myself. In her mind, having experienced real starvation, how could anyone do this to themselves? There were real people in the world dying of hunger; didn't I know how lucky I was to be living in a world where food was plentiful? Of course I did, and felt suitably guilty, ashamed. I tried to hide it as much as I could, stopped going swimming, wore layers and layers of clothing to cover up how thin I was, pretending nothing was wrong.

Anorexia got in the way of who I was meant to be. My parents, my tutors, my managers, my agents, they all wanted me to remain a child—it was easier that way, the eternal, pure Min, the set-up as it was meant to be, the innocent and the master. They didn't want puberty or teenage angst. They wanted the little girl with a winning smile. I didn't have the energy to fight back.

What I could do was keep it under control, not let my weight drop below a certain point. (That's not quite true. For a few weeks, with my mother away in Korea, our father in charge and not a clue what to do with me or my sister, my weight plummeted.) But most of the time there was an acute self-awareness that I didn't want to be hospitalized. Anorexia became my best friend and for a time seemed to replace my violin as the focus of my affection.

And the trouble is, once you reach that state of mind, it's very difficult to step out of. You're starving. Your brain is starving. Your illness, your desire for nothing, becomes the closest thing to you, the friend you can talk to, the friend who listens. You hide this friend from your parents, from your teachers, from your friends. It understands you, and, paradoxically (though they could never admit it), it understands them too. For they can see it, see it hiding, pretend it isn't there. It's just like those games of hide-and-seek you played as a child, where everyone knows where you are, but says nothing. Anorexia is doing what they want and what you want. Who else are you going to listen to?

It's still hard to talk about, which is why it comes now, and isn't running through the story. I'd put it away, like I put away so many things. It seemed normal at the time, what one did, the price you paid. There was always a price. I knew that much, but when you're young it's so easy to see it in the frame of "Well, that's what life is." You don't know any better. And then suddenly you do.

How did I get out of it? I fell in love, remember! I fell in love with that inappropriate boy. Adult instincts, adult needs. Adult Robert got me out, Robert who only wanted me to be ordinary. Robert banished anorexia and Robert got me back on the violin, two things in one unsuitable youth! Well, thank heaven for him! He wanted a normal girl. I wanted to be normal too—still do, but know I am not. Talent is a burden you can't throw off. It can drink or drug you to death. It can depress you into suicide. But you can't have the talent surgically removed, the weight of it. Only with death do you part.

6

Months went by. I was approached by an old colleague to become artistic director of a company that was organizing musical evenings for actors and singers. It seemed a good opportunity to be still a part of music but acting behind the scenes. Life wasn't going to be where I had imagined it to be, but at least it was life. Though I was still practicing, I missed playing the concertos. My arm still had the stretch, my fingers still the memory, but the muscle was cut off from the heart. Managerial work was all very well, but after a while it made no real sense. It wasn't me.

I was beginning to see that there were two Mins now, Min with a violin and Min without a violin, and that they were one person. There didn't have to be a choice. There was a world outside the violin, and a world inside the violin. I'd talk to friends. Maybe they didn't know it, but they started massaging that heart, coaxing it back to life.

Somehow I was turning myself around, so that I was facing a different way. There was a path ahead. It was long and steep and I was standing on it. I had a violin in my hand and it was good. I wasn't strong, but I could get stronger. There were boulders in the way, but I could climb over them. I wasn't sure I'd make it the first time, yet I could keep on trying. Friends would catch me when I fell. But falling was going to be OK. I knew how to get up now. I didn't want to take it quietly anymore, shrink back, pretend nothing had happened, that everything was all right. Everything has been all right for far too long. And the idea came to me then: that if I put it down on paper, if I tried to make sense of it, tried to make a whole out of these tumbling fractures, then I could, not walk away from it, not "move on" as we're all told we must do, but absorb it, let it settle in my bones, something that has happened, that will always have happened, that now is a part of me, a part of my whole as much as anything else. I could look at myself and think, "Yes, there stands a violin player. An unstrung player, but a player." I had a set of strings now. It was time to attach them to something. I started writing.

2016. It's been over a year since my violin came back and it was sold. I still have the other one, the one I bought with Matt in New York. Up till now, I've been thinking, "I won't do anything real with it, because I'm going to get my old violin back." But now I know I am not. Someone else has it. He may not be able to bring it to life, but it belongs to him (and his consortium). He's proud of it well enough. I've seen pictures of him, showing it off as if he's caught it, like it's a prize fish, knees bent, arm thrust out, a look of victory on his face. He's won! (He won't call it by its rightful name, the Kym Strad—following the tradition of naming Strads after their owners—preferring the Euston Strad, an unhappy name with unhappy associations.) Does he think about it night and day? Would he die with it clutched in his hands? Probably not. Keeps it safe? No doubt about that. No Pret A Manger while he's in charge.

Does he play it? I believe so. Does it play how it should play? Of course it doesn't. I don't think he has the means for that, the hand, the eye, the ability. One day I hope my violin will find itself back in the hands of a true player. That's what it was made for. I have come and I have gone, as the new owner surely will. My Strad will live on. Perhaps its time has yet to come. I hope so.

But I am not as certain about that as I used to be. Times are changing, have changed. Violins like my Strad are not bought to play as they once were. They are bought as an investment. They sit in safes, lie locked up behind fireproof doors and impregnable security tumblers. They are brought out, handled with white cotton gloves, turned reverentially, examined, admired, then returned to the prison of safety. They do not earn their keep in the concert hall. They earn their keep in the dark. And the more of them that are bought for this life, the more they are shown and examined and returned to the dark, the fewer come onto the market, and the fewer on the market, the greater grows the price when and if they do. And who buys them? Not violinists. We can't afford a Strad anymore, no matter how good we are. But Stradivari made his violins for players. A great Strad can fill a big concert hall like no other violin. They have a power that no other instrument can match. They were made for playing, for bringing the great concertos to life, made for traveling with their partner from concert to concert, in trains and airplanes, lying on the back seat of cars or by a weary bed. They were made to be heard in the world! Yet there they lie, spirited away, gagged and alchemized, glowing in the dark. That is their fate now. And when they are played (if they are played), it's a mere tinkering at their edges, a travesty of their talent. And for us musicians? Well, we are in a sort of dark too.

But I have this violin, and it is this violin I have to deal with, have to come to a sort of realization about. I have never really bonded with it and we all know why—when my violin came back, and I wasn't able to keep it, I held this one at a distance, not physically, or ever consciously, but there was a blockage, as if I was holding something that didn't quite fit, that didn't look right.

I have been playing it for a good many months now and, although I am getting to know it, I am still filled with conflicting emotions. It has a lot to offer, I know that, know too that I have not been very fair to it, its presence always a reminder of what it is not, what it could never be, a suspicion too that it is always trying to wheedle its way into my affections, for it is a pretty thing. But it's a Stradivarius, made with knowing hands. It was one of his favorites. If it hadn't been damaged, it would be among the very top league of Strads. It deserves to be played, it deserves a *player*, as much as any violin.

But recently I have been able to look at it with a more dispassionate eye. It's partly because I am beginning to see myself as a player again, and as a player I have to look at an instrument and think, "What can this do for me? What are its strengths? Where are its faults? Could it play this, that?" And for a long time my thinking has been conditioned by both violins: the one that is gone, the other that lies in my hand. Now other shapes are forming on the horizon, shapes which, as each day passes, come into sharper focus.

Not long ago Charles Beare showed me another Strad. I held its sheen, I heard its voice. The air cleared a little, like a mist lifting, for I heard what I had never heard from the violin I own now—the vast clarity of a Strad, its unadulterated purity. And it made me think of what I had, what I lost and what I have replaced it with. I realized that if I hadn't been so broken when it was shown to me, I would never have bought my current Strad. Buying it was a mistake—a mistake in oh so many ways. It led me closer to the people I should have kept away from. I should have listened to other dealers. They had offered better, dispassionate advice. But I had devils in my ear, and their language had latched on to all my fears. So I'd ended up buying the wrong instrument, and the worst thing that could have happened did happen—my violin was found and I had not the means to bring it back home. Had I bought a Guadagnini . . .

So it was a mistaken purchase, this violin, the rider to a false dawn, leapt upon at a time when I wasn't thinking straight, when others were thinking for me. Does that sound ungrateful? Cruel? Could it have ever worked for me? Haven't I imposed upon it a burden which it can never throw off, that I will never let it throw off? There is, I am sure, an element of that. But I have tried with it. But hearing that other Strad made me understand that my current violin is never going to work, not for me, not for who I am, who I want to be. I am beginning to need a violin that I can rise to. It's not as if I haven't been working on this one. The bridge has had a lot of attention. The sound post was a little too short and has been replaced with a better fit. But I am beginning to think, unless a solution to the big problem is found soon, it might be time to move on.

I didn't think that six months ago. Had Charles not shown me the other Strad, maybe it would have taken me longer to come to my musical senses. But then I was shown another violin, an Amati. The Amatis are a family of luthiers going back to the 1550s. Andrea Amati had made violins for Lorenzo de' Medici, Catherine de' Medici and Charles IX of France. He was succeeded by his sons Antonio and Girolamo, known as the Brothers Amati. They introduced many innovations in violin design, the summit of their achievement perhaps the perfection of the F-holes. Girolamo had a son, Nicolò, who went on to be the greatest of the Amati luthiers. His violins possessed a power far beyond those of his father and uncle, and it was he who had as his pupil the young Stradivari.

This violin hadn't been played for nearly fifty years—a beautiful instrument, far finer than the one I currently own. We were both worried that its sound would be too confined for my needs. But it told me one thing. I'm looking for the right partner.

Aren't we all.

A lot has happened since I wrote that. The police showed me stills from the CCTV. I'd been avoiding them, avoiding seeing what it looked like, this moment that nearly sank me, but with all these words under my belt I felt lighter, suddenly able to take them on board, keep afloat. They came in a little folder, the insignia of the British Transport Police in blue and red, the inscription "Pan London CCTV Hub" printed underneath. It was how I imagined a sales document to look like, nicely presented, the binding punched so the pictures flip over one by one, lazily or quickly, you can take your pick. There weren't many and the first few are of me and Matt.

Picture number one and there we are walking along the platform, just off the train. There's a couple in front of us, another couple busy with bags to the side, but there we are walking along, Matt on my left, me with the Strad slung over my shoulder. The picture is blurred but our demeanor is unmistakable. We are not happy. We are walking in separate worlds. My head is down. Matt is staring ahead. I don't want to read too much into it (though it's difficult not to) but it's clear we're going somewhere I, at least, don't want to be. Picture number two and here we are again, moving up the platform's incline. Matt looks so much bigger than me, so much stronger, his stride more purposeful. He's carrying more than me, bag, wheelie, his cello strapped to his back. I just have the violin. Just the violin. Next frame, and we are outside Pret. I can count five people directly outside, and a few other brave souls on the periphery. Otherwise it's a wet and abandoned concourse, empty tables, empty seats and a discarded newspaper on the floor near the camera. We're looking in at the warmth inside. We're about to go in. The picture is taken by camera no. 6454 FCT and the time is 20:19:30.

I flip over. Now it's 20:52:44. We've been in Pret for thirty-three minutes but the picture is not of us, it's of the thieves coming out onto the concourse. There are three of them. Two to the left of center, the brothers, and to our right, their uncle, tiny, tiny, tiny. He barely comes up to the lead boy's shoulder. He wears gloves. The boy has his hands in his pockets. What do they look like? Can I gauge anything from them? The boy in front is looking straight ahead, but

the uncle and the brother behind ... they seem to be looking, eyes on everything around them. Yes, that's it. They're
scanning as they walk. Next picture they're as we were, about
to go into Pret. I can't see myself but I am on the other side
of the window. It's 20:54. Perhaps they've already seen me,
clocked my expression, perhaps I have seen them looking in.
I have no memory of it, but all that stands between us is a
thin sheet of glass and the intent of our lives. Collision time.
They will be convicted for what they are about to do, and I
will have to serve my sentence too—am still serving it, good
days, bad days.

20:59 and it's all over. The camera at the back of the building catches them coming out. The burlier of the two lads is
out in front, best foot forward. The little uncle behind. He
has a coat draped over something. Behind him chairs are
stacked up. In the picture, blurred, they look like bones of
a skeleton, the flesh, the body, the soul, all gone. In a couple
of seconds I'll have woken up. In a couple of seconds I'll be
rushing around, screaming my head off inside. In a couple
of seconds everything that I thought I knew will be stripped
bare, my life just a skeleton, stacked up, unusable, a terrible
winter beginning to envelop me.

I couldn't have looked at those pictures when I started
this. That ice age has gone. And my life is warmer now, no
longer shrunken, huddled, fearful, the ground I stand on no
longer barren, inhospitable.

A couple of months back, I went down to see the owner, a
close friend of mine, about the Amati. A series of lucky events
had led it to be in his possession, but he is not a violinist. It
had been sitting in a cupboard, largely unplayed, for decades.

That's not to say it had been neglected. He'd spent the many years understanding the care such a fine stringed instrument needs, and although unused, it was in superb condition. The original label pronounced it a "Brothers Amati," which was assumed to mean that it had probably been made by a pupil of Nicolò Amati. But Charles Beare was utterly intrigued by the instrument. He thought the shoulders looked like Nicolò's work. It had the *feel* of a Nicolò.

Charles asked the owner if he could spend some time with it, take a good look. Of course he could. He sent it to the lab for the wood to be analyzed, dated. Many violins of value have their provenance examined in this way. It's a sort of fingerprint, can help identify not only a time but also a place, a workshop, a man. The information that came back was astounding. They'd discovered that the wood that made up this Amati came from the same piece of wood that Nicolò went on to use on a number of his more famous violins. So this unsung Amati is in fact the work of Nicolò's early hand, most likely when he was still working in his father's work-shop. The Brothers Amati label was simply slapped on—at the time a common practice, merely indicating the workshop in which you're working. This is wonderfully liberating news.

Thirty years? It emerged that it hadn't been played for the best part of a *hundred*. The Sleeping Beauty of violins. It was extraordinary. The owner, delighted, excited by the prospect, said, "We'd love you to wake it up."

So, I drove down to play it, took my current violin with me too. Now there was my current violin and there was this one. I was still debating the idea of how I should approach my current violin, worrying that whatever we did wouldn't be for me. Now I was venturing on to the possibilities of the Amati. There was the worry that, however good, the Amati was not, and never could be, a soloist's violin, not one that could carry the sound in front of a full orchestra and out into the auditorium. You need a voice for that. It isn't about size, it's about construction. (When they were recording her, Dame Eva Turner, the legendary opera singer, used to have to stand at the *back* of the orchestra, otherwise she would drown everything else out!)

I took it up and played it.

It was like magic, a wand over, a spell broken—and yes, I guess that kiss too. I was breathing life into a voice, a set of lungs, a heartbeat that hadn't been touched for decade upon decade. The more I played on the Amati, the more it opened up. After an hour its voice was beginning to be heard, the warmth, the quality—it was just starting to clear its throat, flex its muscles, work away the cobwebs.

All the parts are original, it works in the way Amati intended it to work—so I have in my hands something special again, something to hold, to nurture, something to let swim into me as I swim into it. It's life again and it feels amazing.

It was probably played quite a lot at the beginning of its lifetime, but I have the opportunity of bringing it into the modern world. That's not as crazy as it sounds. Its set-up is not exactly old-fashioned, but it has a bridge and fingerboard made from pieces of highly sought-after wood and ebony, once readily available but now almost extinct. It is a testament to the age and preservation of this beautiful violin. It is whole, undamaged and radiant. After years of coaxing and, dare I say, healing a succession of damaged and vulnerable violins that have been through innumerable wars, for the first time the boot is on the other foot. It's the violin that's undamaged, the player who needs the healing.

～

I played everything I was working on. And everything I played sounded better. Ah, there's that disloyalty again! But I can't escape it. More than that, I have to face it. And what the Amati did for me, when I drove away, was something that hadn't happened since my violin was stolen. I was disappointed not to go home with it. I wanted to take it back with me, play it again. Again and again.

The car was rolling down the motorway. There were lights ahead and lights behind, lights too in my head. I could feel motion within me. My mind was traveling, wide awake. There was no end to this ride. I could live with this violin, open it up, let the music roll. It would lead me places. We would travel together and it would lead me places. We could cover new ground. I could commission a new piece, a young composer, a wiser Min and a perfect violin. There is so much we could do, free, unfettered, full of joy. It was bubbling inside of me.

The key to music, to Min, had been unlocked. I'd got my excitement back.

CODA

A FEW NIGHTS AGO I PERFORMED IN PUBLIC FOR THE first time. It wasn't anything big, just a dinner at a private house. Some of the guests I knew, most I didn't. I played in the dining room, the guests seated around the table, their first course waiting in front of them. A couple of the guests up at my end had to get up and stand back. There wasn't room enough for them and me and my Amati (and using that phrase, "me and my Amati," is a first for me too).

It had to be a simple thing for me to play, nothing too heavy. There was a dinner to eat, talk to pursue. I chose Dvořák's *Humoresque* No. 7, one of the pieces I'd heard Kreisler play all those years ago, when I was young and little and had thought that playing my violin would make me forever happy, that it would always be enough. Dvořák wrote the *Humoresque* while on holiday in Bohemia with his family. He'd been living in America for a couple of years, but in this so-called break began collecting material for the cycle of what were originally piano pieces. He wrote the outline for the first *Humoresque* on July 19, 1894, completed the whole score just over a month later in August. They were immediately popular (in the United States, No. 7 became the setting for a mildly risky verse concerning the toilets on trains), had been a favorite of mine as an example of Kreisler's magical touch. Reading this, you might think you don't know it, but let me assure you, you probably do. The *Humoresque* carries one of those melodies that appear to have existed forever. As soon as it starts you recognize it. It bears that rare gift that certain refrains possess, a kind of harmony that has always lain out there in the ether, just waiting to be captured, written down, played.

I had played it many times in my youth. Now I was playing it again. The sound filled the room, filling the spaces, the music almost pushing itself up against the guests, wrapping itself around them. The Amati was built for bigger rooms than this, and yet, in the past, this is how violins such as this must have sounded when played in those drawing-room soirées in Vienna and Salzburg and all over Europe. This is how Schubert would have heard much of his own music, Beethoven too, all of the greats, not just the pattern of notes, their phraseology, their argument, but the physics of the thing, the bow on the string, and the vigor of the players, music with real intimacy.

And there I was, standing in a modern replica of those times, playing it in front of these few people, their faces turned toward me, and me standing in the doorway, on the cusp of going in or staying out, the sound of the *Humoresque*, enchanting one moment, sad, reflective the next, a call to something, a memory that you never had but could feel as history in your bones, almost like ancestry. That's what it was, my past flowing out and my future too, all hope and sadness, all regret and joy there on the strings and under my fingers, my arm and my bow and the lungs of the violin filled with all that had gone before, all that lay ahead, released into the air. I was playing again, there were people listening. I was doing what I was meant to be doing, what I was born for, for that's the truth of it, I was born for it, not taught, not learned, but born for it, born like Ricci was born, like Kreisler, like Heifetz. Big names, yes, bigger than mine, but like them a name with no choice in the matter, just a violin before us and our hands stretched out to hold it. This was just the beginning.

And now I am playing the Brahms again. It's the same Brahms and yet it isn't, for the Min playing it now is not the Min you might hear in that recording. I have changed. Cruel things have happened to me, things, dare I say it, which I didn't deserve, but for which I bear sole responsibility. I trusted people I shouldn't have trusted. I didn't listen to the people I should have listened to. I had a mother and a father, and I didn't know them well enough, as they didn't know me. Something had got in the way.

Blame it on the violin? Not at all. Don't blame it on anyone. It happened. I was born in Korea. I bowed to my father, took my shoes off before I ate. I played a tune and won a prize. I found my violin. I listened to the wrong man. I was a little Korean girl thrown into a strange world. I was asked to perform without quite knowing who I was. It's still a strange world, and I am still Korean, but I don't bow anymore. I know who I am. My Strad is gone but I can still hear the call of it. My Strad is gone but I can play again. I have memories of the Strad and the Strad will have memories of me. When it is played again, out in the open, on stage, in front of an audience, it will remember me. It will open its heart and remember me.

My name is Min.

I play the violin.

ACKNOWLEDGMENTS

I am truly grateful to friends, family and colleagues who have given me such huge support and encouragement: my mum, dad and sister, Min; to Ian, Tim, Sally, Chris, Celia, Simon, Andy and Tony.

Heartfelt thanks and appreciation to my wonderful agent Annabel Merullo, whose care and unwavering support I cherish. To my marvelous manager Maurice Whitaker, who helped me find myself in the first place. To Caroline Michel, Jonathan Sisson, Rachel Mills and all the fantastic people at Peters Fraser and Dunlop—including, of course, Marlowe, whose gorgeous doggy greetings I look forward to every time I visit.

I am incredibly grateful to Venetia Butterfield at Viking, whose kindness and encouragement gave me strength to persevere with this journey. To the exceptional team at Viking— Chris Bentham, Helen Eka, Nicola Evans, Tom Monson, Cathy Packe, Anna Ridley, Ellie Smith and Lindsay Terrell.

Special thanks also to Molly Stern for her tremendous support and help in bringing me and my book forward. And to the amazing people at Crown—Chris Brand, Kevin Callahan, Jon Darga, Lauren Dong, Sally Franklin, Roxanne Hiatt, Meghan Houser, Rachel Rokicki and Rebecca Welbourn.

ACKNOWLEDGMENTS

I am eternally grateful to the most brilliant and patient of editors, Joel Rickett and Rachel Klayman. It is a privilege and joy to be inspired and guided by you both.

And, finally, my deepest and greatest thanks to Tim Binding, who helped me find my voice in the first place and without whom this book would never have been written. I am forever indebted to your boundless generosity, spirit and genius.

ABOUT THE AUTHOR

Born in South Korea and raised in the UK, MIN KYM began playing the violin at the age of six. At sixteen, she became the youngest ever foundation scholar at the Royal College of Music; at twenty-seven, the first recipient of the Heifetz Prize. The legendary conductor Sir Georg Solti praised her "exceptional natural talent, mature musicality, and mastery of the violin." Her Sony recording of the Brahms Violin Concerto with Sir Andrew Davis and the Philharmonia Orchestra was released in 2010. She lives in London.